D1549878

A MEMBER OF THE HODDER HEADLINE GROUP

For my daughter Elly, with love

Orders: please contact Bookpoint Ltd, 78 Milton Park, Abingdon, Oxon OX14 4TD. Telephone: (44) 01235 400400, Fax: (44) 01235 400500. Lines are open from 9.00–6.00, Monday to Saturday, with a 24-hour message answering service. Email address: orders@bookpoint.co.uk

*British Library Cataloguing in Publication Data*
A catalogue record for this title is available from The British Library

ISBN 0 340 80421 1

First published 2001
Impression number   10 9 8 7 6 5 4 3 2 1
Year 2007  2006  2005  2004  2003  2002

Cover photo from Corbis Images.
Typeset by Transet Limited, Coventry, England.
Printed in Great Britain for Hodder & Stoughton Educational, a division of Hodder Headline Plc, 338 Euston Road, London NW1 3BH by Cox & Wyman, Reading, Berks.

# CONTENTS

# FOREWORD

Welcome to …

**Hodder & Stoughton's Beginner's Guides to Great Works**

… your window into the world of the big ideas!

This series brings home for you the classics of western and world thought. These are the guides to the books everyone wants to have read – the greatest moments in science and philosophy, theology and psychology, politics and history. Even in the age of the Internet, these are the books that keep their lasting appeal. As so much becomes ephemeral – the text message, the e-mail, the season's hit that is forgotten in a few weeks – we have a deeper need of something more lasting. These are the books that connect the ages, shining the light of the past on the changing present, and expanding the horizons of the future.

However, the great works are not always the most immediately accessible. Though they speak to us directly, in flashes, they are also expressions of human experience and perceptions at its most complex. The purpose of these guides is to take you into the world of these books, so that they can speak directly to your experience.

## WHAT COUNTS AS A GREAT WORK?

There is no fixed list of great works. Our aim is to offer as comprehensive and varied a selection as possible from among the books which include:

* **The key points of influence** on science, ethics, religious beliefs, political values, psychological understanding.

* The finest achievements of **the greatest authors**.

* The origins and climaxes in **the great movements** of thought and belief.

* The most provocative arguments, which have aroused **the strongest reactions**, including the most notorious as well as the most praised works.

* The high points of **intellectual style**, wit and persuasion.

## READING THIS GUIDE

There are many ways to enjoy this book – whether you are thinking of reading the great work, or have tried and want some support, or have enjoyed it and want some help to clarify and express your reactions.

These guides will help you appreciate your chosen book if you are taking a course, or if you are following your own pathway.

### What this guide offers

Each guide aims:

* To tell the whole story of the book, from its origins to its influence.

* To follow the book's argument in a careful and lively way.

* To explain the key terms and concepts.

* To bring in accessible examples.

* To provide further reading and wider questions to explore.

### How to approach this guide

These guides are designed to be a coherent read, keeping you turning the pages from start to finish – maybe even in a sitting or two!

At the same time, the guide is also a reference work that you can consult repeatedly as you read the great work or after finishing a passage. To make both reading and consulting easy, the guides have:

* Boxes identifying where we are in the reading of the great work.

* Key quotations with page references to different editions.

* Explanations of key quotes.

Our everyday life is buzzing with messages that get shorter and more disposable every month. Through this guide, you can enter a more lasting dialogue of ideas.

George Myerson, Series Editor

## A NOTE ABOUT QUOTATIONS

Quotations are taken from the translation by A. Tille, revised by
M. M. Broznan, J. M. Dent & Sons, Everyman Library, 1933.

Passages are cross-referenced with two widely-available editions:
Penguin Classics, translation and introduction by R. J. Hollingdale
(Harmondsworth, 1969) and the Viking Portable Nietzsche,
including a complete text of this work, edited and translated by
Walter Kaufman (Viking Penguin, New York, 1954).

In the body of the guide these editions are referred to as '**P**' and '**V**'
respectively, along with the relevant page numbers, and *Thus Spake
Zarathustra* is abbreviated to *TSZ*.

## SPECIAL FEATURES

This Beginner's Guide aims to bring to life the reading of this great
work, and to put that reading in context. For this purpose, a number
of special features are included in the text:

❉ *Quotation Boxes*: These frame a small number of short passages
   that are of special significance within the guided reading. They
   are given particular attention as points where major steps are
   made in Nietzsche's strange evolution of thought.

❉ *Key Concept Definitions*: Throughout the reading, but especially
   in the early stages, key ideas are picked out for special definition
   under this heading.

❉ *TSZ* is an extraordinarily prolific work, with a dizzying play of
   argument and vision. It is important that our reading follows this
   work in its multi-dimensional unfolding, rather than closing it
   down artificially to a single line of development. There are a
   number of '*Summary Boxes*' where different dimensions of the
   reading are focused. The most important are:

   i. '*Nietzschean Therapy*': These shaded boxes identify and
      summarise the psychological and emotional struggle that
      makes Parts I–III so dynamic and intense.

   ii. *'Zarathustra's Modernity'*. These shaded boxes identify and summarise the experimental thread of Nietzsche's art, which gives the book its radically modern quality.

   iii. In Book III, the focus increasingly shifts to the unravelling of the complex doctrine of 'Eternal Return', for which a sequence of shorter unshaded 'Summary Boxes' is provided, to keep track of the intricate argument. The same device is used to convey the rapidly moving drama of Part IV.

Bullet points are used to give clear summaries of the progress of our account, and chapter boxes will enable you to locate easily the movement through Nietzsche's text.

We hope the result will be a flowing discussion that fills in difficult points for you without too much interruption.

## A GREAT WORK: FRIEDRICH NIETZSCHE'S *THUS SPAKE ZARATHUSTRA*

The nineteenth-century German thinker Nietzsche has been one of the dominant influences on modern thought. His work offered a radical challenge to orthodox morality and religion, and he proposed startling new concepts of human nature, language and society.

* For Nietzsche himself, *Thus Spake Zarathustra*, written in 1883–4, was his major achievement, his 'new land'.

* Adopted and distorted by the Nazis, *Thus Spake Zarathustra* has subsequently inspired many eminent thinkers who have found in it the sources of a way of thinking that is adapted to the modern condition.

* This book is unique in its mixture of philosophy and story-telling, analysis and poetry.

* Concepts such as 'the superman' and 'eternal return' continue to perplex and inspire new interpretation. These ideas have been able to take on rich new meanings over the decades, and can still speak to the present. Yet many have also found them offensive or absurd. This is arguably the most provocative book in modern culture.

* At the book's heart, Zarathustra remains one of the most intriguing characterizations in modern literature: recluse and teacher, therapist and convalescent, poet and rigorous critic.

# INTRODUCTION:
# PHILOSOPHY AND THE WORLD

## CAN PHILOSOPHY CURE THE WORLD?

Nietzsche's *Thus Spake Zarathustra* is a masterpiece of **therapeutic philosophy**. Throughout this book shines Nietzsche's belief that his ideas may cure his readers of their otherwise hopeless condition. Without this book, these readers will have no hope at all of ever recovering. However, the aim is not simply to cure some individuals – Nietzsche sees the whole world as sick, and his philosophy as the only hope of progress.

These seem extraordinary hopes, perhaps the product of an unbalanced mind, and Nietzsche was indeed, in the years 1883–4, in an extremely heightened state of tension. But it is important, before leaping to biographical conclusions, to recognize that other major philosophers had also believed that their thinking might cure readers of a sickness and, in this sense, make the world better. This therapeutic hope is one of the most deeply rooted philosophical motives. You can find it being expressed by Socrates, the philosophical voice of Plato's dialogues, written in the fourth century BC. The Roman thinker Cicero, an inheritor of the Greek ideal, would have been outraged to hear a philosopher propose other valid reasons to write philosophy, or even engage in philosophical discussion. In our time, the therapeutic ideal of philosophy has been both recorded and defended by the eminent American thinker, Martha Nussbaum.

*TSZ* is poised on the brink between philosophical lucidity and personal madness, but one can also see this book as the last great work in an ancient tradition, the last classic of therapeutic philosophy.

In modern times, philosophers have become more professional. They have not usually justified their writings as making anyone better, some thinkers have written to correct a widespread error of thought; others to try to expound a new system; to give a foundation to science, to religious belief, or to moral values. Many have written to criticize or explain the ideas of other philosophers. More engaged thinkers have tried, through their writings, to understand a political or social crisis. As political theorists, philosophers have offered to provide support for new political forms, like democracy or national sovereignty or the city state. They have written to expose the logic of the free market or to explain its necessity, to endorse beliefs such as human rights, or condemn the misuse of language in common public debate. Major philosophers have provided theories of grammar or explained the wider significance of new scientific theories, like evolution or relativity. Few modern philosophers have dared express the hope of curing any sickness, individual or social.

Is *TSZ* then a backward-looking book, a last gasp, before the age of sober and professional philosophy? The roots do go deep into western and also eastern thought, and it is hard to understand *TSZ* out of the context of *ancient* traditions. But in other ways, Nietzsche's book is profoundly modern. Many readers and critics in the twentieth century found this work anticipated or even prophesied their own concerns, their anxieties and also their need for new forms of expression. For a modern critic like Karl Jaspers, writing in the shadow of the rise of Fascism, *TSZ* contained the germs of a modern state of mind, the angst and the uncertainty, but also the energy and courage of the modern. Certainly, *TSZ* anticipates the questions asked by twentieth-century and twenty-first-century philosophers. Where do our moral values come from? Why do different societies hold differing beliefs? What is the role of language in forming our values? How does the individual achieve a coherent self in the face of the complex flow of experiences? What is the connection between the body and the self?

As we will see, Nietzsche's strange book embodies an ancient hope, therapeutic philosophy, in a modern form, and with modern attitudes. The whole text is also ambiguous in mood. For alongside its profound hopefulness, and even idealism, there runs a current of bitter pessimism and even cynical despair. Every moment of hope is answered by a caustic irony, every enthusiasm by a deep defeatism. Certainly, this is not a book with a happy ending. Having constructed a web of hopes, Nietzsche seems to use the final part as a travesty. But then again, within the mockery, new idealism shines through: the ambiguities of *TSZ* are as boundless as those of experience itself.

## THE EXPERIENCE OF READING *THUS SPAKE ZARATHUSTRA*

There is a basic problem about how to read the book. Few philosophical works have so directly expressed the personal experience of their author – the fear of madness, the depth of isolation, the risk of fragmentation. This is a book which readily lends itself to being read autobiographically. Yet it has at its centre a fictional character, Zarathustra, and every idea is thoroughly worked into the fictional scenario. So you can also say that few philosophical books have made it as difficult to determine their author's point of view.

As you read *TSZ*, you are confronted by a flood of sayings, metaphors, symbols, characters and stories. At the centre is this enigmatic character called Zarathustra – a sage, a mock biblical prophet, a modernist poet – to whom most of the sayings are attributed. Around him are arranged other voices: the saint, the townspeople, the tightrope-walker, the disciples, the dwarf, the wizard, and the ugliest man. Certain questions confront any reader. What *kind* of book is this? Is it philosophy, or politics, or poetry, or fiction, or a sort of home-made religion? How seriously are we meant to take the individual statements, many of which are individually famous or notorious? Do the characters represent ideas or viewpoints? What meaning is this book meant to have?

In addition, over the whole experience of this book, there hangs a historical ambiguity. Many humanist, liberal and radical thinkers have loved *TSZ*: from the existential socialist Karl Jaspers in the 1930s to the liberal feminist Martha Nussbaum of the present day, from the French radical theorist Michel Foucault to the anti-totalitarian novelist Milan Kundera. Yet this same book was adopted in the Nazi period as an honoured ancestor by the Fascists, who saw in some of its concepts, notably the superman, a source of their own ideology. In the high tide of Nazism, the philosopher Martin Heidegger proclaimed Zarathustra's announcement that 'God is dead!' as the wisdom of the new age of the National Socialist revolution.

In this guide, we will be pursuing the understanding of *TSZ* as a vision of individual struggle towards well-being and freedom – in the tradition of Jaspers, Nussbaum and many others. However, over this text of therapeutic hope, there still hangs the historic shadow of its appropriation by totalitarian ideology.

## OUTLINE OF THIS GUIDE

This guide examines *TSZ* as a whole, focusing on some of its most influential ideas. Throughout, we will be considering how Nietzsche attempts to give a modern form to the ancient hope of therapeutic philosophy – making people better by a distinctively philosophical education. This will also involve considering the ironies which Nietzsche continuously showers down upon his own deepest hope, his own dearest project. If you think *you* have doubts about the therapeutic possibilities of philosophizing, you can be sure they are nothing compared to Nietzsche's own rage towards his own ideals. This is a text with a divided soul.

The chapters are as follows:

Chapter 1: *The Life and Times of Nietzsche.* The ambiguities of the life, and the path to the work.

There then follows a guided reading of the four parts of *TSZ*:

Chapter 2: *The Prophet and the Superman.* A reading of Zarathustra's Introductory Discourses, the first section of Part I. The first encounter with Zarathustra, and his earliest teachings.

Chapter 3: *The Sickness of the Human Spirit.* A reading of Zarathustra's Discourses, the main body of Part I. The analysis of the sickness afflicting the human condition, and the role of morality in sustaining that sickness.

Chapter 4: *Suffering and Redemption.* A reading of Part II as a journey towards new teaching and self-awareness on the part of Zarathustra. His theory of the 'will' as a source of redemption.

Chapter 5: *The Gateway of Being.* A reading of Part III centred on the concept of 'eternal return' which Zarathustra proclaims as his particular doctrine, the relationship between time and freedom in *TSZ.*

Chapter 6: *The Final Ambiguity.* A reading of the later stages of Part III and Part IV examining the strange encounters with the 'higher men', the lost and needy souls of the book's ending.

Conclusion: *The Spirit of Zarathustra.* A concise review of the significance of *TSZ* since its appearance and throughout the twentieth century.

# 1 The Life and Times of Nietzsche

One fact dominates the story of Nietzsche's life, in retrospect. In December 1888, at the age of 45, he had an irreversible mental collapse and died in 1900 without recovering mental or physical health. This last phase has cast its shadow over the whole story, the whole achievement of this great and original mind. To what extent are the ambiguities and complexities of his work really symptoms of an impending personal collapse? *TSZ* was Nietzsche's own most valued work. It is also the expression of a time of deep crisis in the years 1883–4. How does this vision of sickness and well-being relate to the tragic life of its author?

The main sources used for this brief account of Nietzsche's life are Karl Jaspers' *Nietzsche*, which includes a classic account of his life; Ronald Hayman's *Nietzsche; A Critical Life*; and R. J. Hollingdale's *Nietzsche's Life and Philosophy*. Quotations from Nietzsche's letters are taken from Jaspers and Hayman.

## THE EARLY YEARS

Karl Ludwig Nietzsche married Franziska Oehler on 10th October 1843. He was a Lutheran pastor and a dedicated scholar but already, at the age of 30, he was unwell. Their first child Friedrich Wilhelm Nietzsche was born on 15 October 1844. On 10 July 1846 his sister Elisabeth was born: she was to be perhaps the closest person to this often isolated soul. Then on 30 July1849 their father died. Softening of the brain was diagnosed. Sickness and death haunt Nietzsche's earliest years.

Nietzsche's early childhood is itself a story of writing, reading, illness and isolation. He was sent to the local school but then gained a place at the elite academy of Pforta in 1858. By 1862, we find the young

Nietzsche already recording his doubts about the religious faith that dominated his home background. He was turning even then to ideas of evolution, and already had begun to speculate on the human condition: '...*we scarcely even know whether humanity itself is only a step.*' Jaspers remarks that '*Nietzsche philosophises as a boy*'.

## THE FIRST PHASE OF A PHILOSOPHICAL LIFE

Nietzsche was certainly an intense boy, often lonely and absorbed by ideas. In 1863, we find him already struggling to convey the mass of his thoughts on paper: '*I stare for a long time at the white paper in front of me, troubled by the confused crowd of themes.*' This sense of 'abundance' is one of the experiences given to the character Zarathustra. His story can be traced to these early years.

The older schoolboy summed up his life in three terms: '*I drink and eat and write.*' There is a paradox about this writing. On the one hand, it reflects an intense desire to communicate; on the other hand, it is part of an experience of isolation. This sense of a personal quest deepened when Nietzsche went to study theology at the University of Bonn in 1864. It was at this time that the young man visited a brothel, which may have been a source of possible infection leading to the illness of his later years. Others have seen this ill-health as inherited from his father, and some have insisted on its psychological basis. For later interpreters, as for Nietzsche himself, his life is inseparable from the question of illness.

In 1865, Nietzsche went to Leipzig as a student, where he shifted to the study of classical philology, the ancient languages and their origins. Already he saw his own future in learning and teaching: '*My goal is to become a truly practical teacher ...*' This desire to teach is another of the central characteristics we find in Zarathustra, alongside the struggle to communicate and the sense of isolation. It is as if Nietzsche's whole life were a preparation for that character and his story.

Nietzsche was searching for fellow spirits and in 1865 he discovered in a bookshop the major work of Schopenhauer, *The World as Will and Representation*. For the student Nietzsche, this book by his older contemporary was a mirror of his own thoughts and struggles. Throughout his life, Nietzsche needed heroes of thought, models for his own quest. As Jaspers notes: '*Schopenhauer becomes* the *philosopher for the young man.*' Under this dark influence, the student wrote home to his sister: '*Do not take it so lightly, this existence …*' In *TSZ*, Zarathustra must struggle to overcome a figure called 'the Spirit of Gravity', who seeks to drag his thoughts ever downwards. Maybe Nietzsche himself had to struggle for his own lightness, out of these early years.

In 1867, he was not only in the army, but was also still studying. Now Nietzsche was acquiring other heroes, such as the ancient Greek thinker Democritus whom he saw as having travelled 'systematically through everything knowable'. In 1868, Nietzsche was reading and writing about the late eighteenth-century German authority Kant. At the same time, he suffered an injury to his breastbone from an accident, and the motif of ill-health begins to make itself heard more distinctly in his life.

## THE SECOND PHASE OF A PHILOSOPHICAL LIFE
In 1868, Nietzsche met the composer Richard Wagner whom he described as '*a fabulously vivacious, fiery man*'. Later he wrote that '*Wagner was the most complete man I ever knew.*' A new hero had arrived in his life. This was an extremely vibrant moment for Nietzsche. In 1869, at the age of 24, he was appointed Professor of Philology at the University of Basel in Switzerland. He then took Swiss citizenship as required by his employers, though this did not stop him serving with the German army as a medical orderly during the Franco-Prussian war in 1870.

Amidst the energy and early success, there is always a note of darkness. In 1869 Nietzsche was feeling '*the ash-grey cloud of loneliness*' which never left him. In his job, he was lecturing to a mere eight students. At the same time, he introduced seminars, as if looking for some other kind of discussion, some different form of teaching. This concern is to be at the heart of Zarathustra's life; how to teach, when to speak? One of his colleagues recalls Nietzsche as a lecturer, quiet and appearing weary, but with a voice that 'came from the soul'. This is the voice towards which Zarathustra will struggle.

In 1871, Nietzsche started work on what became his first book, *The Birth of Tragedy*. At this point, he tried to become Professor of Philosophy at Basel, instead of specializing in Philology, and failed. He was never to satisfy the criteria of orthodox philosophy. In the same year, he found a publisher for his book, Ernst Wilhelm Fritzsch, who was also Wagner's publisher. This book examined the origins of Greek tragedy 'in the spirit of music' and developed a more general theory of a conflict between different human potentialities embodied in the rational Apollo and the ecstatic Dionysus. On reading the book, Wagner wrote to Nietzsche: '*I have never yet read anything more beautiful than your book!*' Nietzsche's struggle to communicate his ideas had begun.

In 1872, we find Nietzsche lecturing in dialogue form, with fictional characters, in an attempt to convey his new ideas about Greek philosophy. His educational passion shines through in these years. He was also lecturing on 'an authentic German educational establishment'. At the same time, he was also discovering in the mountains a landscape which he declared to be 'my nature', a landscape that also belongs to Zarathustra.

### THE THIRD PHASE OF A PHILOSOPHICAL LIFE
Nietzsche's thought was becoming ever more radical, his position more isolated. In 1873, in a book on the influential thinker David Strauss, he attacks the ideal of a German Reich as an enemy of true culture: '…*in Germany there no longer exists any clear conception of what culture is.*' This Nietzsche had to be heavily censored before he could be adapted or distorted to meet the needs of the Nazi period.

At this time, Nietzsche also made one of the crucial advances in his thinking, in a now famous essay called 'On Truth and Falsehood in an Extra-Moral Sense'. Here he asked himself '*What, then, is truth?*' and gave the reply: '*A mobile army of metaphors …*' Here begins a new approach to language itself, and Zarathustra is a kind of climax of this preoccupation with metaphor, with the creative role of language in shaping the world.

By 1874, Nietzsche was privately voicing criticisms of his hero Wagner for developing 'no individuality other than his own'. In 1875, he met Paul Rée, a medical man and philosopher. Rée was to be a major figure in the next years of Nietzsche's life. Five years younger, he was already the author of a work on *Psychological Observations*. Nietzsche's friendship with this German-Jewish thinker marks another part of the break with Wagner, for whom anti-Semitism was a dominating attitude.

Amidst all the creativity, the shadow of illness was darkening. Headaches were common, and by 1875 Nietzsche was certain that he was '*afflicted with a serious brain disease*' (**H**: 183). Out of this dark time, he produced a retrospective celebration of his hero Wagner, entitled *Richard Wagner in Bayreuth* (1876), to celebrate the opening of Wagner's new theatre. But his own ideas had moved on. He was planning a 'school for educators' with Rée.

In 1877, Nietzsche was working on *Human, All Too Human*. This massive book employed a new style, full of separate sayings and paradoxes. While he was consulting new doctors about his feared brain disease, he was also finishing this study of human nature that abounds in modern insights and questions:

*'Of First and Last Things'*

*… how can something originate in its opposite, for example rationality in irrationality, the sentient in the dead …*

*We behold all things through the human head and cannot cut off this head.*

This book seems to deepen the sense of strain. While writing Part II in 1879, Nietzsche recorded that '*Teaching causes me too much mental strain*' and in May 1879 he submitted his resignation in Basel.

The new book was not a public success at the time. By 1879, Part I had sold only a hundred or so copies. But intellectually, the project was alight. He carried on into a visionary sequence entitled 'The wanderer and his shadow', which contains a painful vision of '…*that shadow all things cast whenever the sunlight of knowledge falls upon them*'.

## THE FOURTH PHASE OF A PHILOSOPHICAL LIFE

From 1879, Nietzsche became a traveller. In the next year he moved from Italy to Naumburg, back to Venice, to Marienbad, to Switzerland and the lakes, to Genoa. By 1881 we find him in St Mauritz. He was seeking a climate for his health but was also driven by intense loneliness. All this time, he was writing what have become major works in the development of modern thought. The first notes on what became *TSZ* were written in August 1881 in the Swiss Alps. The irony of these years is well summed up by Jaspers: '*Nietzsche's passionate desire to communicate did not prevent his loneliness from increasing …*'

Nietzsche's thinking continued to broaden at this time. This was a time of great intensity for him, when he found his own experiences almost too strong to bear: '*The intensity of my feelings makes me shudder and laugh*,' he wrote. Soon he was engaging with current scientific ideas of the conservation of energy, ideas which reappear within another of the key themes of *TSZ*, the strange conception of eternal return. He seems to have felt himself on the verge of a breakthrough but also unable to advance or communicate: '*I am not yet mature enough to deal with the elementary ideas I want to present in these final books*,' he wrote to his friend Gast. At other times, he felt he had a message for humanity: '*Believe me: the peak of all moral contemplation and work in Europe … is now with me*.' This may sound like a delusion, but in this particular case the delusion has seemed convincing to many subsequent thinkers and historians.

Into this difficult time there came another crisis, Nietzsche's relationship with a young woman called Lou Salome. They met in Rome in 1882 and an intense triangular relationship developed with Paul Rée's involvement. It was to Lou Salome that Nietzsche began expounding the themes of *TSZ*, including the notion of the main character. He explained to her that he had picked on Zoroaster as his philosophical ancestor because this Persian sage was the original theorist of good and evil, the first to conceive an afterlife determined by the moral value of a person's being on earth. This was the vision which Nietzsche now set out to overturn, and so Zoroaster–Zarathustra was to be the voice of the next era, when morality was to loosen its ancient hold.

However, the relationship was unstable. By 1882 Lou Salome was denouncing Nietzsche as a madman. Yet at the same time, she declared to Rée that Nietzsche was to be 'the prophet of a new religion'. This is the surrounding emotional environment of *TSZ*. By 1883, the relationship had ended and Nietzsche wrote with painful self-awareness: '*As soon as I had merely dreamed this dream of not being alone, the danger was frightful ...*' This inward turn, or self-analysis, becomes another integral part of the character of Zarathustra.

In January 1883, Nietzsche wrote Book I of *TSZ* in 10 days. He sent it to his publisher on 14 February. There was a dead period for a while, and then in June he was preparing to write Book II. In September he was sketching out Book III and recording that '*poor Zarathustra is sinking into real gloom*'. With an ever-deepening sense of physical illness, Nietzsche moved through Genoa to Nice where, in January 1884, he finished off Book II and recorded his sense of exhilaration in terms that can also be found in the story itself: '*I have never sailed with such sails across such a sea.*' On 18 January 1884,

Nietzsche sent Book II to the publisher and it was being printed by 8 February. The author reflected with triumph and gloom: '*It is possible I am a fatality for all the coming generations of mankind.*'

Another lull was followed by another burst and in July 1884 he was working on Book III. By December he had moved on to Book IV. These volumes were each published separately, with a mere 20 copies of the last part being printed at the author's own expense. The letters of this time reveal an intense awareness, sometimes despairing and often exhilarated: '*I was in a real abyss of feelings, but I raised myself …*' This courageous self-scrutiny is the very reverse of madness, whatever the approaching catastrophe in Nietzsche's near-future. *TSZ* is the expression of a moment of almost unbearable clarity, surrounded by physical illness and emotional stress, but never in itself unbalanced or out of touch.

## THE FINAL PHASE: BEYOND THE PHILOSOPHER'S LIFE

The aftermath of the Zarathustra phase was a time of intense productiveness. Nietzsche wrote in these years a number of his major works, including *Beyond Good and Evil* (1886) and the *Genealogy of Morals* (1887). But the surrounding story is now one of terrible crisis. He was running out of money and his eyes were failing. In 1888, Nietzsche arrived in Turin seeking 'dry air' and experienced a last moment of clarity: '*The clearest October light everywhere … I am now the most grateful man in the world.*' On 15 October 1888, Nietzsche had his forty-fourth and last birthday of sanity.

The last time had begun. By the end of November, he was losing control of his facial expressions. At Christmas, he was gripped by euphoria. From January 1889, the philosopher's life was over: in its place was the invalid's condition. He was taken by his mother to a clinic at Jena University, where he remained for some time, before passing into the family's care.

In 1893 his sister Elisabeth took over control of the books. Ironically demand was rising and now there were new editions. She created a Nietzsche Archive and by 1894 public success had begun, though Nietzsche was never to share in it. In the summer of 1898, he had a minor stroke and on 20 August 1900 he caught his last cold. Nietzsche died on 24 August 1900.

# The Prophet and the Superman

## 2

When Nietzsche embarked on *TSZ*, he was sure it was his great achievement: '*Meanwhile I have written my best book and taken that decisive step for which I did not have the courage last year,*' he recorded as he produced the first part. He declared as the work carried forward: '*The time of silence is past: let my Zarathustra … divulge to you to what heights my will has taken flight …*' Towards the end of the work, he wrote: '*I have discovered my new land …*' Let us now explore Nietzsche's strange journey.

## SETTING OFF

PART I
**Introductory 1**

The book begins with an event, not a proposition or an argument. Nietzsche doesn't start by saying that people have previously believed in, say, experience, but that he will show its limits, or that people put faith in science but … or asking what the origins of language are or the meanings of the state. Instead, this book opens by telling the reader that Zarathustra was 30 when he left the mountain home that had been his refuge for ten years and went back down into the world.

So why start here? Why not begin by telling us what the book is about, what its ideas are, what questions will be asked? And if you are going to begin with a character, then why start with his age? Why not his personality or his interests? In fact, the device is deeply consistent with the aims of the book. Nietzsche is not setting out just to make us think about the world or criticize general theories. He is going to demand that every reader engages with their own experience. Zarathustra is many things, but he is always a way of demanding that we take philosophy personally.

## Meeting Zarathustra: initial aims

Nietzsche had the following aims for the reader on meeting Zarathustra:

✳ The reference to 30 years makes you think of your own age, and pushes you towards autobiographical ways of reading.

✳ Are you older? Are you younger? The starting-point raises the question of experience and wisdom.

✳ You might well read this differently if you come back again when you are older.

✳ The ideas which follow exist relative to *his* age and to yours. They never float free of human time. This is the reverse of a timeless philosophy.

To read *TSZ* is to enter upon your own inquiry, into your own life. From the start, we are being invited to think about the character in terms that will instantly become comparable to our own situation. No one is going to be able to read this without bringing in the question of their own age. The book, therefore, begins by drawing us into a personal engagement, the kind of comparison we are more likely to make between ourselves and the hero of a novel. We are, in philosophical terms, going to be taken on a journey into **reflexivity**.

> **ZARATHUSTRA'S MODERNITY**
>
> Reflexivity: The book is an early example of the inward turn of modern thought, whereby all thinking is a form of self-questioning.

In addition, at least three other subjects are being introduced. First, there is the general question of **time**, which will be an obsessive preoccupation of Zarathustra. As you check briefly on your own age, you show yourself in passing that you too share this obsession. Human beings are obsessed with time: it is the most normal anxiety, and the most pathological. Second, there is the question of **authority**.

Would you take seriously a man of 30 who is just leaving this remote home? Is this someone you would trust to cure or help you? Would you accept this voice? What would you require instead, if not? Here, perhaps, it is also suggestive that Jesus lived for no longer than 30 years: is this the age of authority? Third, there is the issue of **home**, leaving and returning. The whole issue of origins, roots and home-coming runs though the text, often to the accompaniment of intense ambiguity.

As readers, we are given a connected sequence of events and characters. Yet, in other ways, it is hard to take the narrative seriously in the way you would if you decided this was a novel. We do not really seem to be invited to exercise much curiosity about the people we do encounter; they remain nameless, and largely faceless. We learn, for example, little more about Zarathustra's previous life. He springs up into the moment of leave-taking and sets off. Is this fiction? Is it allegory – a set of events and figures who stand for an underlying argument? Is it a mockery of story-telling? Here, too, Nietzsche is on modern ground.

Perhaps there is just enough story to enable the book to establish its central therapeutic concerns. The therapeutic project is what links *TSZ* with the worlds of fiction – where, especially in the nineteenth century, the idea that a book might help or even cure its readers is much more familiar.

## ZARATHUSTRA'S MODERNITY

Ambiguity of genre: Genre is the 'type' of text: lyric, poem, epic, novel, tragedy, dialogue, and so on. The classics of modern writing often defy definition by genre. Like *TSZ*, they do not fit a previous type. For example, Joyce's *Ulysses* is a realistic novel but also a mock-epic parody of Homer; Wittgenstein's *Philosophical Investigations* is both a series of remarks and a systematic argument.

## AN INCURABLE SPIRIT

PART I
**Introductory 2**

As he comes down into the world, Zarathustra's first and most famous encounter is with a figure called 'the saint', who is 'an aged man'. There are meetings like this in the nineteenth-century Russian novels of Dostoyevsky, and shadowy figures enter his fictions apparently to personify viewpoints or psychological extremes. Still, this meeting is more like a moment in Bunyan's seventeenth-century *Pilgrim's Progress* than in Dostoyevsky's *Crime and Punishment*. The figures hardly pretend to be individuals.

However, you can say one thing about the saint – he is certainly a sick man. He lives in a way that, for Zarathustra, is clearly profoundly out of touch with reality. And this isn't simply a matter of false beliefs, say, or philosophical errors. He is a deluded soul and his behaviour everywhere shows signs of this condition.

Replying to an inquiry from Zarathustra, the saint declares that he spends his time in his forest singing songs and that:

> QUOTATION
> *I make songs and sing them, and making songs I laugh and weep and chant: thus I praise God.*
> cross reference **P**: 41; **V**: 124

This is an eccentric life, isolated and apparently marginal. In fact, the saint is the first representative of the world's sickness, in an acute form. He is the beginning of what we shall call the 'Nietzschean therapy' of *TSZ*. Here the sickness is first defined – though not the cure.

Throughout the book, Zarathustra confronts, and maybe shares, the threefold sickness: repetition, non-communication, self-annihilation.

**NIETZSCHEAN THERAPY:**
DIAGNOSIS
*The world's sickness*

* First, this is a repetition sickness. The sufferer only ever does one thing: here, he sings monotonously.
* Second, this is a sickness of non-communication. The saint is so convinced he is praising God, that he never notices he is not

Thus far you could say this is also a plausible case study in a character who has lost touch with reality: the kind of old man you might see mumbling on a park bench. But of course, he is labelled a saint, which is why he stands for something more than a personal illness. He is the representative of what others would call 'faith' and as such he is also the beginning of the conflict between Zarathustra and 'the religious'. The saint's sickness is bound up with his religious calling.

The saint stands for what in modern thought can be called the **Other-centredness** of religious being. His life is lived in relation to this Other which he calls God. It is this Other-centredness of being which is the deep sickness in the context of *TSZ* as a whole. The book is a profound analysis of the ways in which western thinking and culture creates and nurtures the sickness of Other-centred being.

Sainthood is the condition of total self-surrender, absorption at every minute in the being of the Other, whom the saint calls God. This life represents the history out of which arises the continuing sickness of the world, which is everywhere still under the sway of such values, even if the beliefs themselves have faded:

talking to anyone. So his songs shade into talking and laughing to himself.
* Third, this is a sickness of **self-annihilation**. The saint simply has no sense of how his behaviour appears from the outside. So deep is this unaware-ness, that you could say the saint has no self at all.

## NIETZSCHEAN THERAPY:
DIAGNOSIS
*The sickness of faith*
* The actions of 'faith' are purely mechanical, these are songs without meaning outside the dream of the believer. They depend for this sense of self-justification on their religious reference.
* This singing is both routine and ritualistic. Ritual here means sacred repetition.

## ZARATHUSTRA'S MODERNITY
'Self' and 'other': These are key themes of twentieth-century thought. Following Nietzsche, Sartre, for example, continued to confront the struggle of the 'self' in the face of the power of the 'other'. Later thinkers include Laing, in psychology, and Foucault, in cultural theory.

Other-centredness: In all these different philosophies, there is a threat of Other-centredness, of being overwhelmed by an outside presence, failing to live a life from the inside.

---

QUOTATION

*But when Zarathustra was alone, he spoke thus within his heart: 'Can it indeed be possible! This old saint in his forest has not heard that God is dead!'*

cross reference P: 41; V: 124

---

As yet, there is no hint of the curative aspect of the project. Zarathustra, the embodiment of therapeutic philosophy in later stages of the book, makes no attempt to engage with the saint. He is a hopeless case. Here we see an early example of Zarathustra turning aside from a dialogue which he regards as impossible. The saint is 'undialogical', in the language of twentieth-century linguists: you cannot talk to him because there is no possibility of any to-and-fro movement. He is sealed inside his delusion. In this respect, the saint represents a prolonged interruption in the dialogue of the West that began with Socrates.

We can already see *why* no dialogue is possible with the saint. He lives entirely in relation to this Otherness called God, and so he has no 'I' with which Zarathustra could converse. When Zarathustra talks to himself, he addresses his heart, inwardly, and consciously. He speaks to and from a centre: he is capable of being self-reflexive, carrying out an interior dialogue. The saint mutters to himself, deluded that he is addressing another being. He has substituted God for his own centre of being, and so he has no inner dialogue, and therefore he is also inaccessible to the voices of other real people.

If there is no self to respond, then there can be no dialogue. Total self-annihilation is incurable by dialogue. This idea in fact anticipates, and sets the terms for, one of the main controversies in the history of

**NIETZSCHEAN THERAPY**

*The principle of dialogue*

※ There is no cure without dialogue.

※ There is no dialogue without two strong 'I's to converse.

psychoanalysis and psychotherapy. Are there people whose madness runs so deep that they are inaccessible to the process of dialogue?

## A PHILOSOPHICAL VISION

Zarathustra goes down to the town. In the marketplace he finds a crowd waiting to watch the performance of a tight-rope artist. Should we take the story literally? There is no detail, nothing concrete or specific. Weird happenings intervene. The effect is more like a dream than a novel, a philosopher's dream or nightmare.

| PART I |
| Introductory 3 |

Zarathustra announces to the crowd that he has come to teach them, and his lesson has a name: **'the superman'**. It is hard to take this as a solemn representation of good teaching. The crowd are not ready. They are waiting to be amused or excited. The declaration that Zarathustra is going to *teach* them seems absurd in that context, and his abrupt announcement that today's lecture is about the superman, an unknown figure, makes no sense to anyone else. As we will see, he does indeed fail to connect. Yet the therapeutic project must depend upon communication, on teaching as communication. If you want to make people better with your ideas, you must first convey those ideas to the right audience. This scene seems to dramatize how not to go about that communicative aspect of therapeutic philosophy.

The teaching is bound to fail. Yet its content is authentic: the superman remains a central idea in the book. So this dream, or nightmare, shows something important about therapeutic philosophy. It isn't enough to announce the right ideas, you have to create the relationship with the audience within which those ideas can take root.

One could see a more bitter irony; if the crowd only want to see a clown, then there's no point in giving them a philosopher. In that case, the scene stands for the inevitable failure of the whole project of therapeutic philosophy in the modern world. Certainly, the scene anticipates some angry moments in twentieth-century philosophy, where thinkers denounce the world for failing to attend. The most famous example is the work of the German thinker, Theodor Adorno, on whom Nietzsche was a strong influence.

In the unfolding story, the key point is that ideas in themselves have no therapeutic power or capability. It is only through a certain kind of communication that ideas – however true or rich – could have such potential. This is a similar kind of insight that emerged at the same period in the early writings of Freud. The same quality of insight can be traced back to Plato and is also found in the earlier nineteenth-century thinker Kierkegaard.

> **ZARATHUSTRA'S MODERNITY**
>
> There is an opposition between philosophy and a **popular culture** dominated by:
> * entertainment and spectacle;
> * mass audiences;
> * the marketplace.

This way of thinking is still alive in the influential theories of Jürgen Habermas, the dominant contemporary philosopher of communication.

The whole episode represents a question that must have troubled Nietzsche. It is, in other words, a self-reflexive moment. What would it mean to teach 'the superman', or any other idea of that kind? How can such a conception be taught? We are on the path to Zarathustra's theory of teaching, a strand of his wider therapeutic philosophy. Even the most eloquent speaker (or writer) cannot teach such a new concept in the form of statements. There is an element of parody or mockery towards the presentation, which simply confronts the audience with a slogan and associated demands. Yet we can already glimpse the outlines of the superman.

> **NIETZSCHEAN THERAPY:**
> **THE PHILOSOPHICAL CURE**
>
> *Communication and cure*
> * Ideas alone have no therapeutic power.
> * Cure depends on communication.
> * In a hostile culture, philosophy cannot cure anyone.

The superman is not an abstract theory. To think about this figure, or idea, means to try to live beyond the limits of life as they are currently felt. To learn the superman means to act against current human nature. During the 1930s this concept was taken over by German Fascism and turned into a pseudo-philosophy of superiority. However, it is clear that no such meaning attaches to the superman in Nietzsche's usage. This is no symbol of racial or any other group supremacy. On the contrary, the superman is a potentiality towards which all humanity must strive, and which none has realized.

## KEY CONCEPT: THE SUPERMAN

* Negatively, the superman is an anti-religious concept. If a new human being is possible, then man is not a created being, with a fixed and given nature.

* Positively, the superman is an evolutionary idea. Current human beings are not the culmination of life on earth. There is a higher future.

The superman is an ideal, a call to surmount our current condition. This call has nothing to do with being inhumane. It means not settling for, or accepting, the easy view of 'it's only human …' To learn 'the superman' also means questioning one's acts. What are their consequences in terms of the kind of life they are constructing? What are you becoming, or making yourself, if these are your acts?

PART I
**Introductory 3**

Zarathustra also announces that this superman is to be the future of the earth. In R. J. Hollingdale's Penguin version, we are given the added gloss that this figure is 'the meaning of the earth'. Zarathustra urges his audience to endorse this vision, by declaring for themselves that 'the superman' 'shall be' that meaning. Meaning is indeed the central concern of the philosophy which Zarathustra is unfolding. He wants to give his audience a renewed experience of the discovery of meaning in their lives. The superman is a way of talking about this experience of meaning. Nothing could be further from any suggestion of conquest or world domination than this call for a return to the search for earthly meaning! This is a stage in developing a modern therapeutic philosophy, not a political slogan.

Therapeutic philosophy seeks to replace God by the meaning of the earth, rules by the inner experience. To live for God is to deny your own self; to experience meaning is to recover that self.

## NIETZSCHEAN THERAPY:

### THE PHILOSOPHICAL CURE

*The principle of meaning*

※ Meaning is an experience, accessible only from a personal perspective.

※ The philosophical cure is based on giving the audience the experience of meaning.

# The Sickness of the Human Spirit 3

The introductory sequence of Part I has told a story. At the end, Zarathustra has failed to teach the world about the superman. Instead, he has gathered disciples, a small group who want his teaching. In the twentieth century, during the period that has been called 'modernism', many artists, writers and thinkers lived out Zarathustra's story. James Joyce and Picasso, Ezra Pound and Brecht, the great 'modernists', saw their work as ushering in new worlds, and they ended up preaching to their own self-chosen elites.

With these 'Discourses', the focus moves away from the question of how to communicate, the nature of the dialogue or lack of dialogue. Instead we are listening to Zarathustra defining the world's sickness more systematically. Above all, he now tries to *explain* why the contemporary world lacks well-being. He also reflects on why this sickness may be difficult to cure. Zarathustra's Discourses aim to:

**ZARATHUSTRA'S MODERNITY**

Modernism: Zarathustra can be seen as an archetypal modernist. He preaches a radical message, and seeks a wide audience. But his radicalism seems obscure in the marketplace. Instead he preaches to the disciples, the fans, the inner circle.

* define the sickness of the world;

* explain the causes;

* sketch the paths to a cure.

At the heart of the Discourses, as we will see, the diagnosis is stern: the world is sick with morality! But how can morality be a sickness? This seems strange in the climate of the new millennium, when morality is often prescribed by both sides of the political spectrum as the cure for contemporary or modern or future ills. How can society be suffering from morality, rather than from the lack of moral foundations?

## THE WORLD'S SICKNESS (1)

### The triumph of 'You' over 'I'

PART I
**Discourses**
*'Of the three metamorphoses'*

Zarathustra tells a parable of three human states: the camel, the lion and the child. The camel is the spirit which demands to carry the heaviest load through life. This is not in itself to be dismissed, but it is at best a prelude to growth. The camel is the least developed form of heroic spirit, one which seeks instant self-justification. By contrast, the lion demands freedom. But in that quest, there is an enemy, which Zarathustra calls 'the Great Dragon'. This monster embodies the spirit of morality, and the lion, in his search for freedom, must confront this antagonist:

> QUOTATION
> *'Thou Shalt' is the name of this Great Dragon. But the Lion-spirit saith: 'I will.'*
>
> cross reference P: 55; V: 138

The Great Dragon is a first image of the oppression of moral values. This monster addresses each person with a fixed message. Against the 'You' of the Dragon, the Lion stands for an 'I', a first-person choice, an act of will. This is a compressed anticipation of the argument that Zarathustra is going to unfold, an argument against all 'Thou shalts'. The lion cannot actually bring about the freedom of the 'I will', but only strive towards it. The third stage, the child, is the future that lies beyond this conflict between the Dragon and the Lion, a new start, free of the conflict between oppressive tradition and the demand for liberty.

## THE WORLD'S SICKNESS (2)

### Humanity in fragments

PART I
**Discourses**
*'Of a thousand and one goals'*

In his parable of the camel, the lion and the child, Zarathustra condenses his whole challenge regarding conventional thinking about values. He then has to set out his vision more directly. In one of the most influential arguments in the book, Nietzsche, through Zarathustra, presents the existing belief in good and evil as the sickness afflicting the human race, and considers more sketchily a number of possible remedies.

Let's look at the discourse which sets out the diagnosis. The 'thousand and one goals' is Zarathustra's name for all the values which different societies have attempted to impose on their members. In this view, every society has made people live by a fixed code of good and evil, at the centre of which is one dominant 'goal' to live by. There is really a note of mockery about the phrase: how can there be a thousand and one supreme aims? What state must the world be in if we are seeking to arrive at a thousand and one different destinations?

In fact, the heading suggests chaos, rather than purpose, a world where there are too many goals being pursued, each seeming to be important but none fitting with any other. Imagine trying to live your individual life with a thousand and one aims, all equally important and each separate from every other one. Perhaps that is one good way of describing a life that is going wrong, where the sense of purpose has become split up among hundreds of different and even conflicting possibilities. I wake up every morning and immediately besiege myself with important projects, with duties. For Nietzsche, this is the situation of the human race as a whole.

Zarathustra declares that, having travelled far and wide, he has seen for himself how every nation pursues its supreme goal, which it makes the central principle of its own code of values. Some people believe that a good person must always strive to outdo all other individuals, to win every contest. Another nation has commanded that to be virtuous means, above all, to remain loyal to the tribe and be willing to commit whatever acts are needed to serve its interests. Elsewhere, a tradition makes its first rule being the honouring of father and mother. In another nation, a good man must first of all master shooting with bow and arrow, and must never tell a lie: his words must be as straight as his arrows. There are as many supreme goals as nations, and as many moral codes as there are supreme goals.

**NIETZSCHEAN THERAPY:**
DIAGNOSIS
*Global morality sickness*
The human race is afflicted by a 'thousand and one goals', each seeming absolute in its own way, none compatible with any other.

In one way, you could see 'the thousand and one goals' as simply a common-sense modern description of the world. Once we are able to travel and communicate more widely than in less technological times, we soon encounter other societies with different values. In each society, it is a crime to act in ways which elsewhere would be either ordinary or praised. Here being good means saving your money and accumulating personal wealth; there such a life may be regarded as either mad or anti-social. Here being good means to have as many children as possible as soon as you can; there it will be a crime or a deviation:

QUOTATION
*Much that one people calleth good another calleth shame and disgrace.*

cross reference **P**: 84; **V**: 170

On the whole, we have got used to this as a fact of life. It was already becoming familiar by the late nineteenth century when Nietzsche was writing. For Zarathustra these codes are a web of delusion. People have mistaken human codes for absolute laws.

All these different values amount to a kind of chaos, where each society imposes on its members a rule about the main goal of their lives, and where none of these rules makes sense from outside that society. Each regards all the others as either disgraceful or irrational, because they don't conform to the familiar scale of good and evil. There are three main symptoms making up the **sickness of conventional morality**:

### Symptom 1: Non-communication

Everything we say as human beings involves some sense of value judgements. It is impossible for us to understand each other if we cannot make any sense of how the other person is judging the world.

### Symptom 2: Complacency

Each society teaches its inhabitants that they are the most fortunate people on earth, the only lucky ones to whom the true values have been granted as a code to live by. This deadens all sense of inquiry or moral adventure.

### Symptom 3: Irrationality

How can any of these moral codes be absolute when each originates in a local culture or history? It is a sign that people are closing their eyes to their world that they continue to believe that there is something special about their own code, more so than any other.

## CURES FOR MORALITY SICKNESS

Zarathustra wants to set people free from these thousand and one goals. However, at this stage of the story, he has no clear prescription, and his answers seem to encourage several different reactions, which lead in opposing directions!

First, philosophy could simply reveal the truth to people, that their values are only relative not absolute. We would call such a position 'relativism'.

## Cure 1: Relativism

This does not seem to Zarathustra to be in itself a good cure. In fact, there is the possibility that this cure will be worse than the disease, that the remedy will have toxic side effects like other modern wonder cures. Zarathustra believes that all previous and extant societies have had such a moral code. Each people *needs*, it appears, to define its own identity according to a distinct moral vision, to set its own goal and make its own prohibitions. It is possible, then, that despite all the philosopher's ridicule, there is no realistic alternative in practice to every nation, people or society believing in its own values, otherwise, there will be no coherent social life at all.

This is a key example of a wider problem for Zarathustra, and for his author. Maybe there is something useless or even destructive about the philosopher's teachings. Could therapeutic philosophy be a poison instead of a cure? That fear has an ancient history, going back to Plato. It may be that people will have to ignore philosophy, if they want to carry on living effectively. So relativism may be a truth which is useful only to philosophers and not to anyone else. It may be a truth, but it cannot be wisdom, that is, truth with the power to help people to live better lives. This anticipates an aspect of the thinking of some major twentieth-century philosophers, notably Ludwig Wittgenstein. So one possible reaction is to put Zarathustra's insight into brackets, to carry on exactly as before. Maybe any society which was influenced by this awkward truth, that its values are no better than any others, would lose all its energy and collapse. As Zarathustra says, these values express whatever has in the past made a nation 'rule and conquer and glitter'. Perhaps a relativist people would just become weak, prey to its more committed or fanatical neighbours. Is this not one of the anxieties that affects democratic or open-minded countries? But Zarathustra does suggest other remedies.

## Remedy 2: Moral creativity

We could still celebrate the process of *creating* values, determining goals, even if we ceased to accept any specific values as the true ones. Here Zarathustra makes one of his most ringing, and influential affirmations:

---

QUOTATION

*To value is to create … Valuation giveth value.*

cross reference **P**: 85; **V**: 171

---

*You* might value loyalty, *I* might value family love and *they* might value athletic success. All of us do still, potentially, have one thing in common, amidst the differences: we are indebted to someone's original act of founding a code of values, setting a goal by which others can live and judge their lives. In this view, all codes began with a moment's creativity, when a founding spirit took a leap into the future and expressed a supreme good by which that future should develop. In this prescription, the remedy for all those frozen codes would be to celebrate new values, to encourage moral creativity. Zarathustra urges us to regard good and evil as the highest examples of human imagination, rather than as rigid formulae by which to make all our decisions.

This leads on to Zarathustra's largest, and most surprising, remedy. He began with the vision of a chaos of goals. Might the highest remedy of all not be the one which brought an end to the chaos altogether?

### Remedy 3: A common goal

If we accept that we ourselves are the creators of all good and evil, then perhaps we could in time come to share in a single act of creation. This is really a question for Zarathustra at this stage of the story. Could it be possible to create a goal for humanity as a whole? He has no definitive answer, but leaves us instead to ponder the question:

> QUOTATION
>
> *... if a goal be lacking to mankind, is not mankind itself lacking?*
>
> cross reference P: 86; V: 172

Zarathustra is arguing that without a common ideal, there is no such thing as a common humanity. We make ourselves human, in our own ways, by creating visions of good and evil, which give purpose to our lives. So far in history, there has been no shared goal, and therefore no shared sense of humanity. Now Zarathustra challenges us to imagine values which connect peoples into a common world, instead of dividing them into separate worlds. We cannot, of course, imagine what such values would be, and neither can Nietzsche's hero. The third cure hangs in the air, as a question to be explored in the reset of the story, and beyond.

## THE CHRISTIAN SYNDROME

| PART I |
| **Discourses** |
| *'Of love for one's neighbour'* |

In the aftermath of 'the thousand and one goals', Zarathustra launches an attack on the dominant morality in his particular society: the Christian ethic. He denounces the way his society promotes, under the guise of morality, a way of being which has at its heart a psychological sickness. Provocatively, he scorns 'love for your neighbour', which he sees as destructive of human well-being. But what could possibly be wrong about asking us to love our neighbour? First, however benign looking, 'Thou shalt love thy neighbour' is a formula. Like other classic formulae, these words address people as 'You'. Even generous morality gives its instructions in the form of a second-person command: 'Thou shalt', as it was represented in the figure of the dragon. But for Zarathustra all such rules are merely ways of promoting the 'You' over the 'I': in other words, their apparent content is secondary. We receive moral commandments as 'you' (or 'thou' in the language of commandment-speak). They establish a way of living that one can call 'Being-You'. In social history, Zarathustra declares:

---

QUOTATION
*The 'Thou' is older than the 'I'.*
cross reference P: 86; V: 172

---

Every moral commandment is a way of preserving the priority of You or Thou and the subordination of I. The more plausible the appeal, the more dangerous is the formula. But Zarathustra also objects specifically to the *Christian* formula. In his view, there is something wrong with the idea of neighbourliness. The whole neighbour relationship is too oblique for Zarathustra. To see someone as your neighbour is not personal. The whole relationship belongs with 'Being-You', rather than 'I'. Neighbourliness, unlike, say, friendship or affection, is neutral, indifferent and, above all, anonymous.

In fact, neighbourliness is a non-relationship. The whole point of the formula is that this 'love' does not depend on any kind of personal knowledge or connection. You have to love the neighbour whoever he or she is, and whoever you yourself are. This is the ethic of anonymity. Whoever I am must love whoever you are, and no questions asked. For Zarathustra, to treat love in this way is to suck the heart out of all 'I-Being', to make impossible the experience of love on which a self is founded.

This diatribe against Christianity is a good example of Nietzsche's theory of morality sickness in practice. We learn to live our lives from the point of view of the 'You'. As small children, and it is as small children that we are most vulnerable to morality in the guise of teaching, we are taught to be good, which means 'You must love your neighbour', if you are being inducted into the Christian ethic of Nietzsche's society. Then, when you face any situation, you listen to that voice: Thou shalt, and to follow its promptings. According to Nietzsche, this has disastrous consequences. It means the 'I' never enters properly into the situation, and choices are never made from that centre. There is a deep sense in which someone who is acting according to the 'Thou shalt' voice is not really having experience of their life at all – but encountering it as if sideways on, as a set of problems whose answer takes the form 'what you must do in this situation … '

**NIETZSCHEAN THERAPY:**

DIAGNOSIS
*Christian morality sickness*

'Love thy neighbour' is corrupting on two grounds:

* It requires us to relate to our lives in the second person: as 'Thou'.

* It requires us to idealize a 'You-You' bond, neighbour-liness, over all 'I-I' relationships.

This argument with Christianity has, of course, been extremely controversial. But before considering its merits and demerits, we must put it back in the context of the thousand and one goals. Zarathustra is not singling out Christianity, except insofar as it is the authority behind his local morality. Throughout the world, every child receives such a commandment – but they are all different. The result is a world – or a non-world – full of people who never enter into their own lives directly, as 'I', but only obliquely , as an obedient 'You'. There could be no real dialogue or understanding between such I-less beings – they have no centre to communicate from, or towards. Instead, there will simply be a war of conflicting commandments, if there is any contact at all.

PART I
*'Of the virtue that giveth'*

Once again, Zarathustra leaves the social world – he has taken his task as far as he can, at this stage. His parting message to his disciples is to liberate themselves from his own teachings, from any teachings:

QUOTATION
*One ill requiteth one's teacher if one ever remains a scholar.*

cross reference P: 103; O: 190

The perpetual 'scholar' or pupil never goes beyond the 'You' of being taught. This is the key difference, the conflict, between therapeutic philosophy and morality – often disguised as education. Moral educators want their pupils to remember what 'You' must think; Nietzschean therapy, as the modern form of therapeutic philosophy, demands that the pupil takes responsibility and leaves the teacher behind to become an 'I' with its own will.

# 4 Suffering and Redemption

Part II shows Zarathustra re-emerging after a gap. Now we enter a new phase of the project of therapeutic philosophy. Something has changed. In the first attempt, there was more philosophy than therapy, and more diagnosis than cure. Now Zarathustra is on the path to the cure.

## ZARATHUSTRA, THE SELF-ANALYST

> PART II
> 'The child within the mirror'

Who is this child, and what is the mirror? This mysterious heading, to the first section of Part II signals a turn inwards – a concern with self-awareness, self-recognition. Now Zarathustra will talk – and think – more about *himself*, as the agent of this great philosophical mission. In Part I, he seemed to believe that the priority was to get the ideas right. Now he knows he must change the teacher: himself. The shift reflects a deepening therapeutic understanding. The doctrine is not enough – you have to have a way of being a therapist. The most influential therapeutic philosophy – that of Plato – was presented through the character of Socrates. His personal quest supported the general theory. However, in this tradition, being more self-aware makes you a better philosopher, a more coherent thinker, as well as a more effective therapist for others.

Zarathustra has been at home in his philosophical cave. He starts afresh because he has felt wisdom building up inside his mind, until the pressure is too great to withstand. This 'abundance' is painful, and demands an outlet. You can read this in two ways. Positively, wisdom needs to be

### NIETZSCHEAN THERAPY:
#### THE PHILOSOPHICAL CURE
*The principle of self-analysis*
* To cure, you must connect.
* Self-awareness is the source of communication with others.

communicated to others. Negatively, in the absence of communication, wisdom becomes painful, a problem rather than an advantage. In effect, Zarathustra has begun to analyse himself, as well as the world. He now realizes that he has a *need,* and not merely a duty, to communicate his ideas.

The whole book, *TSZ*, is now in the grip of a need to communicate, which begins deep in Zarathustra himself, but also within Nietzsche. Now the hero is an 'I' in search of other people, not just a thinker in search of an audience. There is a very strong aura of what can be called 'I-Being' about this new Zarathustra. He declares:

---

QUOTATION

*I go new ways, a new speech is in my mouth.*

cross reference **P**: 108; **V**: 196

---

The whole project starts from this centre in 'I'. The language seems to follow from this setting forth. He has summoned a new language into being by the sheer force of his personal presence; or by the intensity of his newly found need to communicate.

PART II
*'In the happy isles'*

Zarathustra meets his followers or companions and picks up the thread from his Discourses. He makes no attempt to take over the marketplace. You can only speak to those who want to hear.

The communication is their choice too. That insight has roots in Plato and anticipates Freud. Zarathustra pictures his teachings like figs that ripen and fall, waiting to be chosen by the people below. This metaphor is part of

**NIETZSCHEAN THERAPY:**

THE PHILOSOPHICAL CURE

*The principle of self-teaching*

No one can receive understanding against their will.

the new approach to communication, and to philosophy. There is no way of teaching someone if they do not choose to pick up the figs for themselves. You can only make the fruit as tempting as possible.

## FROM COMMANDMENT TO ADVICE

In his Discourses, Zarathustra identified the threat of the 'Thou shalt' formula. Next, he must find his own philosophical alternative to that logic of morality sickness, with its thousand and one sealed goals. He formulates his own code, but it is not one which anybody could apply to a particular situation or decision. There is no way his disciples, even at their most obedient or mesmerized, will be able to live their lives as pupils of this teaching in the passive sense of constantly hearing the instruction, 'You must' and implementing it without recourse to any first-person moment of being or experience.

Trying to make a positive beginning, the teacher urges his listeners to become creators:

> QUOTATION
> *That which ye have called world is yet by you to be created.*
> cross reference **P**: 110; **V**: 198

To adopt Hollingdale's more concise version here, 'you should create' what would, in a different context, be called 'the world'. This is not a commandment. Instead, it is a piece of *advice* – strongly worded perhaps, but no more than advisory. Furthermore, the listener is being advised to become *more* responsible for their own life, not less so.

**NIETZSCHEAN THERAPY:**

THE PHILOSOPHICAL CURE

*The principle of advice*

❊ Therapeutic philosophy replaces commandment with advice.

❊ Advice seeks to strengthen the self.

*Commandments* seek to fix the 'Thou' of 'Thou shalt'. *Advice* only works when the listener transforms the message from second person to first person – asking 'what would I do?' on the basis of this advice. No one can overcome a specific dilemma by treating 'you should create' as if it were a command. 'You should create' is a command-proof formula. Zarathustra offers his advice as a kind of innoculation against morality, or an antidote to the usual formulae.

Part II contains lots of advice. That makes this section feels odd, if you approach it expecting 'proper philosophy'. There is something too personal, too involved about advice by the standards of mainstream philosophical writing. In context, this advice does, however, have a clearly defined purpose within Nietzsche's wider approach. Advice is designed to occupy the place in one's life where moral commandments used to be.

## ZARATHUSTRA'S ADVICE: RESIST THE SIMPLIFYING LIE

PART II
*'Of the virtuous'*

Zarathustra still formulates his positive advice in the light of what he is against. For example, he expresses his sadness at the prevalence of 'reward and punishment', which are the practical consequences of morality. Reward and punishment address the 'You' in everyone: you must not do that or, if you do this, then you will gain ... These concepts get into the bloodstream. Their effect is to drive out experience, since they substitute themselves for any personal or individual viewpoint on situations or choices.

Zarathustra says reward and punishment are lies that have been insidiously woven into the fabric of life – into the external world of actions and institutions, and even into the inner life of people. In effect, reward and punishment turn us all into liars: we lie to ourselves about our experiences using this logic. We use these concepts to explain our decisions and so look at life as if we were not really living it for ourselves. We also talk and think as if certain consequences were natural or necessary. If someone does this, then that must happen to them. But why should that follow? We must each, in Zarathustra's terms, resist the lure of the easy lie.

Zarathustra wants to challenge the rule of morality. Previously, his challenge was negative, diagnostic. This time round, he has far more to offer, positively: there is the beginning of an alternative discourse to that of good and evil.

One way of describing the story is that Zarathustra changes roles.

Part I Introductory  :  Zarathustra the Prophet

Part I Discourses    :  Zarathustra the Critic

Part II              :  Zarathustra the Adviser

PART II
*'Of tarantulas'*

For the Critic, it would have been enough to savage the old lie. For the Adviser, it is important to make that criticism the foundation of a new beginning. He counsels his audience further, warning them not to trust people who seem keen to punish others. Zarathustra is extending his approach: what began as a criticism of conventional ethics is becoming a general view of human psychology. Do not take these people at face value. Their demand for punishment may seem like a love of justice, fairness, righteous anger or sympathy for the victims of wrongdoing, but their behaviour has a hidden meaning. They are obsessed with the punishment itself; they are the creatures of the moral system and they are the means by which its poison spreads.

## SILENCE AND SELF-EXPRESSION

PART II
*'The Night-Song'*

Alongside advice, Zarathustra also turns to visionary expression. There were symbolic passages in Part I, but they tended to have an explicit point in the argument, like the encounter with the dragon. Advice is more open-ended than critique; and as this developed Zarathustra seemed also to need moments of mysterious self-expression that are more ambiguous than his previous parables. Again, the reader is given the chance to take the active role of interpreter, to come upon the meaning from inside. We are being drawn into the making of a meaningful world: which is the aim of this whole therapeutic philosophy.

'The Night-Song' is a point of self-expression for the teacher, amidst his advice and analysis. In fact, this song seems also to be *about* the inner impulse which demands expression: in other words, the moment is expressive, but also reflexive. Here Zarathustra weaves metaphors which illuminate the philosophical process itself, both from the perspective of the teacher and of the audience:

---

QUOTATION

*It is night: now all springing wells talk louder.*

cross reference **P**: 129; **V**: 217

---

The gushing spring, which may originally have been the fountains Nietzsche heard in Rome, is inaudible amidst the daytime noise, both outer and also inner, the bustle and whir of everyday emotions and obsessions. This night-time silence, however, is not only soothing; it is also a kind of nothingness. These waters speak to the night-time self, the one which is free from the routines of ordinary existence, of society; they also echo in an emptiness that is the ear's equivalent to the eye's abysses.

However you interpret this image, the point is that you do have to interpret for yourself.

## NIETZSCHEAN THERAPY:
### THE PHILOSOPHICAL CURE

*Healing metaphors: Self expression – the spring*

✳ This is a metaphor for communication itself, and for the improvement in communication. A voice can now be heard, which previously was muffled.

✳ Communication is also creative energy.

✳ When does the voice of creative energy sound most clearly? In the night, in the darkness, which is calm, and even empty.

There is no right answer anywhere else in the text. So the poetic mode also seems to be right for Zarathustra. It puts responsibility back onto the listener, the reader: these speaking waters are waiting for our attention. It is as if such passages give the reader practice in creating the world for themselves.

The Night-Song ends with a personal appeal: '*I desire to speak*,' declares Zarathustra as he contemplates the call of the fountains in the surrounding silence. Now he experiences the difficulty of expressing his ideas as a *need* to communicate, rather than as a block in himself, or a resistance by the audience. There is simply too much to communicate easily. Any genuine teaching, implies Zarathustra, will carry within itself this driving need to communicate, and so the project is necessarily therapeutic for the teacher as well as the listener.

Often visionary writing seems inflated or arrogant. But Zarathustra's Night-Song has at its centre a painful self-awareness. Amidst the vision, he holds up again that mirror with which he began this phase of the mission. What the mirror shows is never easy to accept. Yes, the fountain stands for inspiration, for self-expression, but the other side of inspiration is a need to be heard, to communicate with others. The visionary is dependent on his listeners, as well as generous to them. Zarathustra warns himself that his own desire to give such gifts to others may also be a weakness in him, a lack, a kind of 'poverty'.

## THE WILL

PART II
'*Of self-surmounting*'

Passing beyond the vision, Zarathustra now has to expound further what is meant by his central advice: to create your world for yourself, with your own will. He closes in on this controversial concept, 'the will', which is one of the main weapons in his argument against morality. Morality is a way of taking decisions without reference to the individual will. What then is meant by the will and how can it liberate us from the sickness of 'Being-You' into the psychic well-being of the strong self?

Zarathustra says that the object of the will is '*the conceivableness of all being*'. In modern politics, it has become a cliché that we need 'courage ... to think the unthinkable'. (This usually means deciding to do something to someone else for which we can find no real justification!) Zarathustra wants us to find the courage to think 'the thinkable'.

So the will aims to render existence thinkable – to make things subject to our power of thought, in both these ways. If something is thinkable, we can focus on the idea of it clearly. We can also make basic sense of its existence. Therefore, the will is no less than our need to render the fact of the universe comprehensible, or comprehensible enough for us to live there. Religious faith, of course, sought to provide an explanation of the universe which made it unnecessary to depend upon our own individual will to render things conceivable. Why are things here? Because that is what the Creator willed. The will of God instead of our will.

> **KEY CONCEPT: THE THINKABLE**
>
> Things can be thinkable in two ways:
>
> * Something is thinkable if it can be focused coherently in words or images.
> * Something is thinkable if it is plausible that it has come into existence at all.

For Nietzsche, things do not naturally lend themselves to our mental workings. There is no inherent logic by which the universe, as we encounter it, should provide food for our thoughts. It might remain entirely opaque, beyond our powers of interpretation. We must take hold of what we encounter and make it thinkable in our human terms.

At this stage, Zarathustra does not elaborate on *how* the will works such magic, although one way we do this has just been presented. We can render our universe thinkable through the use of metaphor. We take hold of objects, perceptions, situations and use them to express our ideas and feelings by means of metaphor. That is why we can make the spring at night express a feeling we have about communication or about loneliness or the acceptance of the void. Here we can already see how far – how diametrically opposite – Nietzsche's creative will is from any Fascist notion of the 'triumph of the will', the collective assertion of force over others.

## WELL-BEING

Zarathustra puts more and more emphasis upon the curative dimension of his project. Moving deeper into the healing moment, we find a stronger expression of what well-being might mean, for such a philosophy. If the realm of good and evil is sickness, what will well-being be like? Clearly, it will be a first person experience, a realm of I-Being, and at the heart is 'the will', bending existence to make possible the expression of *my* experience. Well-being takes a leap forward, moving to centre stage in the theory.

PART II
'Of redemption'

Standing at a bridge, Zarathustra encounters figures called the cripples, who demand to be included in his teaching, to be cured along with everyone else. They testify to his rising influence over others. Zarathustra replies that they have no need of being cured. He is not to be confused with a faith-healer, or a miracle-worker. He is not going to leave magical evidence of his powers. He is a teacher. Furthermore, those who are confronting him as cripples seem to him to be perfectly sound, sounder than many of the so-called normal ones. It is not, he argues, lacking a limb which makes one disabled. On the contrary, far more common is the over-development of one aspect of a person, at the expense of all the rest of them. So the most common distortion is not the lack of a part, but the excessive development of one: the ability at one specific skill or one particular sensitivity.

Already, Zarathustra has embarked upon his theory of well-being, with this idea about rounded self-development.

The main enemy of whole development isn't lack or disability. Our true enemy is the colonization of the whole by a small part. It is our strength we ought to fear, not our weaknesses: the life driven by musical talent or intellect or appreciation of one experience at the cost of every other.

**NIETZSCHEAN THERAPY:**
THE PHILOSOPHICAL CURE
*Well-being*
* A therapeutic philosophy must have a theory of well-being.
* Well-being is another term for wholeness.

As he explains his approach to redemption, by the bridge, Zarathustra's teaching takes another leap forward. We are beginning to embark upon a full-scale theory of well-being, where previously we had a deepening diagnosis of damaged being. Now Zarathustra weaves together this theme of well-being with his philosophical obsession: time. From this point on in Part II and Part III, virtually everything is re-expressed in terms of our relation to time.

Zarathustra sees 'temporality', the human experience of time, as the key to a healing insight into our lives. Previous centuries might have hoped that understanding would free us from time, and change. This ideal is most famously expressed by Plato and his teaching voice, Socrates. Zarathustra wishes his understanding to root us more firmly in time.

| *Therapeutic philosophy* | Platonic therapy | Nietzschean therapy |
|---|---|---|
| *Philosophical voice* | Socrates | Zarathustra |
| *Time's illness* | Transience | Rigidity |
| *Well-being* | Eternal truth | Being-in-time |

The problem about redemption is always: what are we being redeemed from? To explain what in us needs redeeming, Zarathustra defines his own personal 'burden' in terms of his experience of time's illness.

What is Zarathustra's burden? Weirdly, he claims to be weighed down by two of the three dimensions of time. On Zarathustra's shoulders falls the immense weight of the present and the past. He finds this weight unbearable. We have already encountered the

> PART II
> 'Of redemption'

weight-bearing spirit, the camel, which sought out the most burdened mode of being, in order to feel morally justified. Zarathustra is no camel-of-the-spirit. He rebels against the burden. Yet how could anyone rebel against the past and the present? Are they not simply aspects of experience?

Another striking feature of the burden is the coupling of past with present. Why should these two dimensions belong together? Is the present moment not an antidote to the vista of the past? According to Zarathustra, the contrast is not between past and now, but between pastness, including now, and the future:

---

QUOTATION

*And I could not live, were I not a seer of that which is to come.*

cross reference P: 160; V: 250

---

Against the burden of past *and* presentness, Zarathustra sets the realm of futurity. Why is the future different? Why is well-being a function of his relation to the future?

To be a seer, says Zarathustra, means also to be a creator. If you apprehend the future, then you become the future. In other words, it is in our relation to the future that we can become creators and so enter into the experience of freedom. Presentness and pastness define an experience of fixity or fatality. Zarathustra's theory of well-being depends on the contrast between this fixity of pastness and presentness and the realm of futurity, where we can experience ourselves as creators.

We have seen Zarathustra's view of the will as our power to make things thinkable. Now he tries to subject time itself to his own will. He bends our sense of what time is, imposing through his visionary arguments, his chosen metaphors for 'temporality', for our existence in past, present and future.

| State of health | Sickness | Well-being |
| --- | --- | --- |
| *Metaphor of time* | Burden | Vista |
| *Form of courage* | Endurance | Creativity |
| *Orientation* | Pastness | Futurity |

Through these metaphors for time, Zarathustra is preaching a remedy, as well as a diagnosis: we must live in futurity, rather than in fatality. To turn towards the future, means to experience yourself in a radically different way.

There is still a strong diagnostic strand in the thinking, a re-assertion of what sickness means:

QUOTATION
*'Thus it was': so it is named, the will's teeth-gnashing and loneliest wailing.*

cross reference **P**: 161; **V**: 251

Regarding our lives that way round is both a cause and an effect of ill-health. Pastness sits on our consciousness with a weight for which the modern word is 'depression', and Nietzsche's Zarathustra has been one of the main influences in the formation of the psychological culture within which the concept of ill-being as 'depression' has become popular.

If you live your life facing towards the past, you encounter yourself only as a static figure, always already defined. Memory is a third-person story. You look upon your own actions from outside, as if you were a character in a novel: 'and then she decided … and then she found herself …' For Zarathustra, the present is simply the latest instalment of the past. By the time experience reaches you in the form 'now', it is already fixed, slipping away into the story of the past.

## Example

Imagine a dream-like experience. You wake up abruptly, to find yourself at the wheel of a car. You look around, and see that you are driving along a winding lane, unable to see clearly what is around the corner ahead or (in the mirror) behind. For Zarathustra, your state of being can be defined by the first question that occurs to you. There is Mr Heavy, who immediately needs to know: 'Where have I come from?' And there is Mr Light, who spontaneously demands: 'Where am I going?' If you wake up to the first question, you approach your life in the form of a burden: how on earth did this happen to me? If you ask the second question, you leave space for a future, which you can then choose. 'Where am I going?' means 'where shall I go next?'

Following this example, what you cannot do, as you wake up at the wheel of the car, is to settle for 'now'. Many thinkers have advised us to 'live in the present' as a remedy for the stress of memory and the anxiety of anticipation. For Zarathustra, in this central account of 'redemption', there is no real present to live in. What we count as the present is really a past in the making. If you cast yourself fully into the moment, you find yourself carried away into the past, instantly and at every minute. To ask, 'Where am I?' is just another way of asking 'How did this happen?' These are the passive questions of ill-being, or being ill.

Redemption sounds grand and abstract. We associate it with moral concepts, such as guilt and forgiveness. Zarathustra wants to make redemption thinkable in a new way, and he focuses on little things, even little words. The burden has its catch-phrase – 'it was'.

He counsels us to turn towards the future, but there is a twist in this advice. If we do truly orient ourselves to the future, we will in fact achieve a new relation to what came before, and this is what is now meant by redemption:

---

QUOTATION

*Until the creative Will says unto it [the past]: But thus I will it! Thus shall it be!*

cross reference P: 163; V: 253

---

This begins to sound almost like a grammar lesson. In one way, you could argue that Zarathustra substitutes grammar for morality, but these phrases are really metaphors, they stand for states of mind, ways of living.

**NIETZSCHEAN THERAPY:**

*Healing metaphors*

Metaphor of ill-health: 'Thus it was'

Metaphor of well-being: 'I will it'

You can almost measure your degree of well-being by the extent to which you experience your life from the perspective of its futures. So even when you are thinking back, you experience what went before in terms of *its* sense of the future. Your past takes a new shape. If you break the hold of 'It was' on your past, you open up each moment as a previous version of what the future meant to you. In each moment, you rediscover your own will in action. That was the moment in which I exerted my will in that direction, towards that end. Your life is redeemed when you experience it as a sequence of orientations to the future, as it then appeared.

Traditionally, redemption is moral. To redeem yourself means to 'make up' for past failings, to show that you are better than you seemed. There is a theological version, where to be redeemed means to be saved, to be forgiven your sins and accepted into the chosen, despite your past. For Zarathustra, redemption means the triumph over the burden of the past-present, over all 'Thou shalt' and 'Thus it was'. Instead of 'Being-this' and 'Being-You', redemption means the return of the 'I', the moment of 'I-Being'. Zarathustra calls his theory of well-being 'redemption' to show that it occupies the same space as the moral and religious accounts of making up or being forgiven.

However, Zarathustra is not counselling us to abandon the past, to pretend it never happened. This is no philosophical excuse for escapism. On the contrary, Zarathustra wants a new level of engagement with the past. Here the redemptive theory of *TSZ* comes closest to psychoanalytic or psychotherapeutic thinking. The 'It was' account of the past is always fragmentary, declares Zarathustra. To tell the story as an 'It was' is to ask riddles, to set puzzles. The task of understanding is to create whole stories of the active 'I' in a coherent world.

Zarathustra says that redemption will mean being able to tell the story of the past as an 'I will it' rather than an 'It was'. In other words, what seemed to be happening from outside was all the time an effect of the will, but of the will masked or hidden, or hiding itself, unable to own up to its desires or hopes. Zarathustra's theory of the hidden will seems very close to Freud's idea of the unconscious. There are many differences, of course, the main one here being that Zarathustra presents his redemption in terms of a theory of narrative, two ways of telling the story of your life. But Zarathustra, and Nietzsche, share with Freud the aim of a non-moralizing theory of redemption. It is here that both Nietzsche and Freud offer a truly radical alternative to Christianity and Judaism, as they had been understood by their mainstream proponents.

Yet there is a close connection between Zarathustra's account of redemption and the Christian story of a forgiveness. The 'Thus it was' of depression or sickness leaves a life story in fragments. You can only tell the story in bits, 'a fragment, a riddle'. The 'I will' is the way of telling the story of your life as a whole. The 'I will it' flows through and around all the episodes: it is the hidden connection between what seemed to be scattered instants. In the Christian equivalent, each person is called upon to account for their whole life at the time of Judgement. There is, in both philosophies, an emphasis upon the whole story.

## WORDS OF ADVICE

Zarathustra's concentration on words fits in several ways into the history of modern thought. One direct link is with Freud, for whom it was the little trains of inconspicuous phrases which revealed the hidden workings of the psyche. Here Zarathustra's account of

> **ZARATHUSTRA'S MODERNITY**
>
> WORDS (1)
>
> There is no such thing as an innocent word.

redemption belongs alongside Freud's theory of interpretation: these are thinkers for whom language is never innocent.

Zarathustra's analysis of life in terms of 'It was' and 'I will it' also belongs with another modern philosophy called 'Speech Act Theory'. Zarathustra is not interested in defining terms, in dictionary definitions, he wants to understands what people *do* with words, and what words do to us. Every 'It was' type sentence stands for a defeat of the will, and every 'I will it' construction is a moment of rebirth. The most famous speech act book was entitled *How to Do Things with Words*. True, it was written by the English thinker, J. L. Austin, who was in every way an anti-Nietzschean. He was asking for a more rational, less mystical approach, rooted in everyday values and experience. Nothing could have been less Freudian! Yet the emphasis upon the minutiae of grammar and sentence form has one kind of ancestry in Zarathustra.

> **ZARATHUSTRA'S MODERNITY**
>
> WORDS (2)
>
> Words are ways to do things.

In Zarathustra's approach, the true use of language is the one which accepts our own role as the active agent, the 'I'. The 'It was' construction conceals from us not merely the nature of our life, but also the nature of our relationship to words themselves. There is no 'It'; only a hidden 'I'.

Here Nietzsche is also anticipating an important strand in modern social sciences. The close analysis of language, in this approach, reveals a whole way of life. Zarathustra is setting out to achieve a kind of 'philosophical grammar' of everyday life. In this grammar, every 'It was' construction stands for the renunciation of freedom. There are, of course, a lot of different ways to say 'It was …', to turn life into an external narrative, a sequence of happenings. Society can be analysed in terms of the ways in which it suppresses our lives beneath deceptive grammars, false forms of story-telling. Here Zarathustra is the precursor of modern cultural criticism, which has tried to identify precisely the way in which culture imposes its own 'It was' at the expense of our 'I will', substituting objective-looking explanations for our own experience.

**ZARATHUSTRA'S MODERNITY**
WORDS (3)
There is no story as false as an objective story.

Part II has led from the advice to become a creator, through the warning against reward and punishment, the great lies, to the twin concepts of self-expression and redemption. Through the advice and vision Nietzsche is developing a richer and richer concept of well-being. At its heart, there is the key concept of 'will'.

In the classical origins of western philosophy, Socrates declared that the unexamined life was not worth living. Now for Zarathustra, the unwilled life is not worth living, indeed in a sense it is not being lived at all. You cannot truly be said to will an experience or an act, if you do not understand it. Therefore the life of the will must also include self-examination, insight. That is why without the will, in the realm of the 'It was', everything is a riddle, a part without a whole.

## EPILOGUE

P A R T   I I

*'The stillest hour'*

At the end of Part II, Zarathustra returns home and pauses again in his project of communication, leaving behind even the chosen disciples, let alone the wider audience. He is not yet ready to teach the world. His mood changes, and he feels pulled away from his mission, back to 'seek his solitude'. The part of himself that wishes to carry on is, in effect, a call for his own annihilation:

## KEY CONCEPT: WILL

✳ 'The will' is not a separate part of a person. Will is a way of being whole.

✳ There are two ways of relating to your own life: passively, and through the will. These relationships constitute sickness and well-being respectively.

✳ You cannot experience part of your life through the will and another part passively. Therefore, if you enter into your relation with the future through the will, you must necessarily experience your past and present in the same terms.

---

QUOTATION

*Then again the voiceless words came upon me: 'What matter for thyself, Zarathustra? Speak thy word and break in pieces!'*

cross reference P: 166–7; V: 258

---

Zarathustra feels as if the message of his philosophy has surpassed his own ability to communicate: '*And I answered: "Alas, is this my word? Who am I?"* '

# 5 The Gateway of Being

## METAPHORS OF BEING

PART III
'The wanderer'

Zarathustra sets out again. Each time, it is the same mission, to cure the world's sickness. But every beginning is different, and leads to a new journey. Now Zarathustra advances with a fresh feeling of this being *his* journey, *his* life. We see him in the mountains, and now the hero is himself able to reflect upon the nature of the narrative in which he is being written.

Zarathustra now has a gift of foresight, or what might better be called 'future-being'. It isn't that he knows exactly what is going to happen, but he can tell something important about the future – insofar as it is *his* future. What he can anticipate is the inner shape of his own world. Whatever the outward circumstances, his own life will make him feel as if he is ascending a height:

> QUOTATION
> *… for in the end a man experienceth naught but himself.*
> cross reference P: 173; V: 264

This feeling of ascent is what it will always be like to be Zarathustra. In other words, the landscape in which the story places its character is his own personal metaphor for being. To Zarathustra, the world comes in the form of mountaineering. That is the texture of his experience.

This is an important link in the book's philosophy. In Part II, we saw Zarathustra remaking the idea of well-being, essentially by providing new metaphors for health, wholeness and redemption. Now the link between well-being and metaphor is deepened. Each person has their own way of experiencing being, and that is their individual world-metaphor. If Zarathustra's world-metaphor is mountaineering, then what is yours? Is it, say, flying? Or leaping in the dark? Or wrestling with demons? The mountains which spread out around Zarathustra are more than a landscape, they are his version of the world, of *any world.*

In Part II, Zarathustra advised his listeners that each must make his own world. Now we can see how such worlds are made. When a person recognizes their own world-metaphor, and bends life to fit that model, then they are able to make a world in which to travel forward. Zarathustra's own consciousness makes the landscape through which he can pursue his journey. Those mountains stand, in the terms of the book, for his way of making existence 'conceivable', his way to make his life liveable.

Metaphor is the way of being at home in the world. If you can experience a situation in terms of your own personal metaphor, then it will feel as if it is part of your own personal world, or your particular story. One could even say that metaphor is the language of the 'I'.

Only as metaphor does language become 'mine', my personal tool. Everyone uses words in the same way as names or labels. But as metaphors, words are different for each of us. My way of turning 'mountaineering' into a metaphor is going to be my own, and no one else's.

Zarathustra feels a surge of well-being in his role as 'the Wanderer': he declares that his own 'self' has come home to him. This is

## ZARATHUSTRA'S MODERNITY

*The linguistic self*

In the twentieth century, modernist thinkers and writers rejected the idea that each of us has a 'self' independent of words. Increasingly, our sense of self became dependent on language. Nietzsche's emphasis on metaphor foreshadows the work of thinkers such as Jung, T. S. Eliot, Joyce and Sartre.

probably the most specific piece of therapeutic advice, though it is presented in the form of an example rather than a statement.

This is how to lure your self back home. The deepest contrast is between this self-being and the divided being that is produced by 'Thou shalt' and 'It was'. Metaphor is the voice of the will; the others are the voices of passivity and fixity, of the past and the other.

So Zarathustra sets out on Part III's journey in a state of conscious well-being. This could not be more different from the anxious, though excited, descent into the world at the start of Part I. Instead of leaving home, he is now coming home, and taking that home with him on the travels. The return of the self is also an important moment in the structure of *TSZ*. In the next sections, a new leap occurs. Zarathustra is at last able – or driven – to present a doctrine, a message, which he calls **eternal return**. This theory of universal return is preceded by the coming home of the self. Before eternal return, comes personal return.

The next phase of the teacher's life is ready: **the phase of the doctrine**. Whether this is the moment of triumph, or the beginning of final disaster, remains ambiguous. Approaching the world, with new confidence and a new determination to widen his audience, Zarathustra for the first time makes a systematic explanation of his world view. Is this the teacher's final destiny, to become the mouthpiece of his own doctrine?

## COURAGE TO TEACH

PART III
*'Of the vision and the riddle' I*

The scene changes. Zarathustra is on a ship and he is addressing the crew. Sailors are fellow-spirits, he declares, because they do not need absolute certainty about the future.

They choose to divine (or guess) and refuse to go through systematic calculations. Guessing is personal: it is an assertion of the will, which is what they like. For such people, doing the sums properly is miserably impersonal: the whole point is that such figures are the same for everyone. So these sailors are the right audience for Zarathustra's great revelation of his doctrine: for the first time, he addresses himself to the well-being of an audience, and not to their sickness. Without this shift the ideas could not be developed positively. We would remain trapped in the realm of critique and diagnosis.

In Zarathustra's speech, he tells the audience about his own conflict. He symbolizes this struggle by saying that he faces a malign dwarf, who sits on his shoulder, and whom he names 'the Spirit of Gravity'. When you consider that Zarathustra experiences the world as if he were climbing mountains, you can see why his antagonist should be a spirit of gravity. This spirit is the adversary of Zarathustra's personal metaphor. The dwarf stands for all the energies which hold the mountaineer back. But there is a deeper struggle than that, between the climber and the demon.

It is not so much that the dwarf actually pulls the climber down, rather he offers a strange temptation. As one ascends towards the peak, the drop below deepens. The higher you rise, the more you are surrounded by nothing. The dwarf is that spirit which makes you feel you might be tempted to leap into these infinite, empty spaces. He is more the spirit of vertigo, than of ordinary gravity. In his presence, every abyss beckons: why not fall into this gulf and let yourself go at last? The dwarf distorts *perception*, and makes us see the spaces of our freedom as calls to our death.

Against the dwarf, Zarathustra calls on '*courage*', which he says is the refusal to feel vertigo:

---

QUOTATION

*Courage slayeth even giddiness on the edge of the abyss …*
*Is not sight itself the sight of abysses?*

cross reference **P**: 177; **V**: 269

---

For Zarathustra, courage is the counter-will we exert against our dwarf. Our courage enables us to realize that we can stand firmly on our own feet, that we need not give way to the vertigo of the abyss, that it is only from the perspective of that Spirit of Gravity that the emptiness of the high peaks feels like a danger. Only in despair would one choose to see those precipices as invitations; otherwise, they are signs of achievement: look how high we have come, look how securely we stand!

**KEY CONCEPT: COURAGE**

❋ Zarathustra's courage is the act of will by which we look into the abyss.

❋ Without such courage, no one can see far: all sight passes through the abyss.

❋ Zarathustra's courage is a psychological strength, not a moral virtue.

As Zarathustra continues, no one can see at all without looking at the abyss. There are spaces between all the objects in the world. Normally, we think of seeing in terms of our awareness of these objects, but, in fact, those objects are only accessible to the human gaze within the spaces that surround them, and that connect us with them. Therefore, a person who is afraid of heights will also be blind to the world. In every moment of vision, we experience the limits of our own being, how the world spreads beyond the body. Seeing reminds us constantly that we are mortal. Therefore, no one can see clearly who has not the courage to recognize and accept mortality.

Zarathustra is weaving afresh his positive alternative to morality. He, too, has values but they are not moral values because they cannot be expressed in the form of 'Thou shalt' and a list of rules and regulations. These values exist only in the first person and from the point of view of each individual who lives by them. Courage is a virtue, but in a therapeutic rather than a moralistic sense. We are not commanded to show courage; but without it, the world will make us giddy.

## ETERNAL RETURN: THE END OF ZARATHUSTRA'S TEACHING

PART III
*'Of the vision and the riddle' II*

Now Zarathustra the teacher is ready to make his great leap. He has created a story-world which blends together his self-analysis, his critical argument and his positive advice. This time he can move further and use this world to set out his doctrine. In several ways, you can see this doctrine as 'the end' of all his teaching – the end both in the positive sense of being a fulfilment, and in the negative sense that it seems to bring the truly educative process to a halt.

Zarathustra stays inside the story he has begun, which itself stays within the episode on the ship. The hero now tells how he outwitted the dwarf. With his enemy on his shoulder, he came to a gateway, where two signs pointed along two paths leading in opposite directions:

> QUOTATION
> *'Behold this gateway, Dwarf!'*
> cross reference **P**: 178; **V**: 269

Using this image, Zarathustra now explains to the dwarf why man is infinitely free, why the Spirit of Gravity cannot anchor him in the world of fate and necessity. This 'proof' is the doctrine of eternal return. In this phase Zarathustra uses a different kind of argumentative logic. He takes us step by step on the way to his great doctrine.

Zarathustra tells the dwarf to look along the two paths leading from the gateway. One road stretches endlessly behind, the other endlessly ahead. Each is an 'eternity'. These pathways stand for the past and future. The first, and crucial idea, is that both past and future are limitless. Each is infinitely long. Yet they join at this one point.

There are several key ideas in this symbolic picture. First, there is an idea about time and the 'I'. We are used to the notion that space organizes itself around the individual point of view. Most obviously, the universe itself does not have a left and a right. Things only take the shape of left and right from the point of view of a particular gaze. But, in this metaphor, time is no different from space. The one path stretches behind, the other ahead: but only because of the way we are looking, or the way we have come, or think we have come. The pathways seem to unfold to follow the gesture with which Zarathustra points along them. It is his gaze which creates their trajectory.

## The argument of eternal return: Step 1

*Time uses human consciousness to organize itself into past and future.*

Without the human viewpoint, there is no direction in time. The really central idea, though, is that both paths are eternal, or limitless. The image is devised to convey a sense of the infinite depth of the world. Our experience is framed in terms which are limitless. Every moment of our experience defines itself as a meeting of past and future, both of which are stretching out endlessly and have no final horizon. So this is a theory of human consciousness. To be conscious of yourself is to be aware of the world: without that world, there is no self. You need to place yourself in both time and space to be able to say that you are having experience at all. But that world is infinite, in every direction. In that sense, every moment we are experiencing the infinity of the world.

## The argument of eternal return: Step 2

*The past and the future are infinite.*

Zarathustra then keeps up his argument with the dwarf. The paths are contrary ways through time. They join at the gateway, which is called 'moment'. That is, every moment is composed of warring contraries. This version of experience is **dialectical**, though Zarathustra does not use the term.

> **KEYWORD**
>
> Dialectic: the method of thinking which analyses the world in terms of a progressive unfolding of opposites.

The other great theories of the nineteenth century also saw time in dialectical terms. In Marx's thought, each historical era is constituted by a meeting of opposite social classes. In Darwin's thought, each ecological scene consists of infinitely complex networks of competition between life forms. Nietzsche's theory of the gateway moment is the subjective counterpart of these objective theories, of human and natural history. For Zarathustra, each moment appears dialectical from the perspective of human consciousness. We cannot really say how the gateway would appear if there were no people to read the sign above it: this is a human scene. It only makes sense to think of one pathway going back and the other forward from our human perspective.

By contrast with its rivals, Nietzsche's dialectical theory is subjective – he is defining the nature of human experience and not telling a story about the outer world. Another word for this type of theory is **phenomenology**. But above all, Zarathustra's theory is also therapeutic. The aim of the

> **KEYWORD**
>
> Phenomenology: the theory of the nature of our experience of our own consciousness.

theory of time which Zarathustra is proposing is not merely to describe human consciousness, but to enable us to live more effectively, to outgrow certain beliefs which are trapping us in unhealthy ways of being.

We are about to take a sudden and surprising turn. Just before we follow, it is important to recognize that everything Zarathustra has proposed so far suggests that human consciousness is never static. There are tensely poised energies coiled against one another at the heart of our consciousness. What we mean by a moment is incomprehensible without thinking in terms of those two great polarities, the infinite past and the infinite future. We have no awareness of the world, or of ourselves, that is not woven of these contraries. How could there be anything other than a sense of endless movement in such a consciousness?

Here it is important to take the story into account. Zarathustra is not merely theorizing; he is arguing with the dwarf, the Spirit of Gravity. His aim is to defeat this spirit through his new theory and to show the audience, the sailors, that this spirit has been defeated. Zarathustra now looks back at 'the gateway' moment and recalls those dual eternities on either side of it. If we truly recognize the scale of time, as represented by the two lanes, then we will see it is irrational to think that any such moment occurs only once. He looks back down the lane behind, the past, as seen from his perspective:

---

QUOTATION

*Must not all that can run have already run this road?*

cross reference **P**: 178; **V**: 270

---

The way is endless. The past is infinitely deep. Such a road is long enough to contain any number of instances of this moment, and of every other moment.

We began, in Part I, with the metaphor of man as a rope over an abyss. Now Zarathustra shows his audience how deep the abysses truly are. It is as if this doctrine has been held back until we could cope with it, as readers, and also until Zarathustra was ready to teach it – including in that readiness his having found his true audience on the ship. This idea is dangerous, it has to be handled carefully.

## The argument of eternal return: Step 3

*The past is infinite: therefore, it must have space for every present to have occurred already.*

Zarathustra then turns to the other lane, stretching ahead. If the moment must have recurred before down the long vista of the past, then what about the future? Here we have another key idea. All things are interconnected. If everything is bound to everything else, then it follows that the gateway carries its future with it, every time it recurs in the world. In other words, if one thing recurs, then everything else must also recur. Looking down that future, each moment within it carries its own horizon, and so they are all fixed together.

## The argument of eternal return: Step 4

*If every moment has already occurred, then its future must also have occurred.*

This idea is eternal return – every moment is tied to every other moment, as either its past or its future. Thus, if any one moment recurs, every other moment follows along with it. But time is so infinitely deep that it is irrational to presume that no moment ever recurs, that every moment of experience is unique. Therefore, if one moment recurs, then every other moment comes within it. The universe, as experienced by human consciousness, is ruled by eternal return.

## The conclusion of eternal return

*If all things are interconnected, then if one thing recurs, everything else must also recur.*
*Either the universe is fragmented, or the whole system recurs eternally.*

There *is* a tremendous sense of drama about the way Zarathustra unfolds the doctrine. But why should such a doctrine be therapeutic? Is it not, on the contrary, fatalistic and depressing, exactly the sense of fixity that Zarathustra – and Nietzsche – has been arguing against? Why does this doctrine of eternal return seem to Zarathustra to outwit the Spirit of Gravity and set men free?

One possible answer lies in the dialectical nature of the theory. What recurs is not a block of time, but a gateway, a point of alternatives and openings, above all, of contraries. Nothing can ever prevent that gateway from reappearing, and us from standing once more at in the middle of the infinite conflict. We can never turn aside from our freedom, we stand perpetually at the gateway moment, where the lanes run away and where the world waits for us to confront our future and our past, in our own terms.

In other words, what recurs is our dialectical situation, rather than merely this or that event. Individual happenings move over the surface of this deeper pattern, in which the gateway recurs infinitely. No choice, no action, no failure of ours can ever prevent us from finding ourselves back at this gateway moment. This recurrence is built into the way the universe greets our human consciousness. Time will always be this gateway for us, and we will always be standing there, our gaze turning both ways, the universe empty of everything except our gaze and open to our interpretation. This gateway is the scene of the will, and its recurrence guarantees our freedom, endlessly.

## NIETZSCHEAN THERAPY:

### THE PHILOSOPHICAL CURE

The doctrine of eternal return allows humanity for the first time to contemplate its true freedom: *We are endlessly free because we can never unzip our own human consciousness.*

## AFTER THE MOMENT OF THE DOCTRINE

What does the teacher do once he has explained the doctrine? Zarathustra is now committed to defending his big idea, and to expounding its consequences. This gives Part III a very different feeling from earlier sections. Now there is a sense of a centre. You can see this in different ways. On the one hand, ideas have somewhere to hang together. On the other hand, Zarathustra's own position now seems less fluid and less creative. It is as if the creativity has now been fulfilled. We are now reading *Zarathustra's Book of Eternal Return*.

| PART III |
|---|
| *'Of bliss unsought'* |

There is a happiness, he declares, written into our human condition, which we can never renounce or destroy. Although we can fail to choose it for ourselves in our life, the human condition insists on being a happy one. Fresh from his proclamation of doctrine, Zarathustra defines this 'bliss'. First, he is always *'in the midst of my work'*. In other words, we are endlessly put back at the centre of our own world. This is the law of eternal recurrence. Nothing can displace me from my own world, because I am the one who finds himself again at the gateway where the lanes meet.

In modern thought, there has been a tendency to see humanity as pushed to the margins of being. If there is no God above us, then why should we see ourselves as in any way central to the universe? That was how Darwin's theory, for example, affected many of his contemporaries. But Nietzsche's Zarathustra here provides what he thinks is the remedy. In the idea of eternal return, he believes he is offering the healing insight for modern man. If we take seriously the infinite recurrence of this gateway, we will realize that we are always at the centre of our own world. We do not need a God to make us the centre of being. It is in the nature of our consciousness that in each moment we wake up afresh, in the midst of our own project.

Near to Zarathustra, at the gateway, are always 'my children'. They stand for everything that he has created. He moves to and fro in a kind of dance, stepping towards them, then back again. This dance too has the pattern of eternal recurrence within it. The futures which we have made are always there alongside us. People tend to think of repetition in terms of the past, as if only the present and the past repeat. However, for Zarathustra, the future also repeats, and it repeats as the future of this moment, as the world which is created by him from within the moment. Nothing can ever deprive him of this sense of futurity. Recurrence guarantees that his life will always have this future ahead of it. Zarathustra will endlessly dance to and fro with his own children, reaching out to them, and then pulling away again.

We like to think of ourselves as eventually arriving, perhaps, achieving our goal. But in Zarathustra's universe, that arrival is impossible. Our happiness consists in being always in the middle way, never reaching the end. Therefore, at the heart of this therapeutic philosophy, there is a reinterpretation of happiness itself. It is not simply a way to be happy; it is a new way, in Nietzsche's view, to understand what happiness is. Most therapeutic methods attempt to achieve happiness in new ways. Nietzsche attempts to understand happiness in a new way. For Nietzsche, bliss is 'unsought', it is simply written into the nature of our experience.

---

ZARATHUSTRA'S BOOK OF ETERNAL RETURN

Happiness is the inevitable fact of being at the centre of your own world

---

Happiness is already here, in the act of self-creation; and no other act is possible, as we stand endlessly at this gateway moment.

PART III
*'Before sunrise'*

The doctrine of eternal return is also expounded as a vision of endless beginnings. In our consciousness, the Big Bang is always exploding outwards. Things are, in

Zarathustra's next metaphor, 'baptized' infinitely. Here he turns again to denounce morality: how could moral concepts contain such a universe? How can a world that is endlessly new be confined by a simple duality like good and evil? Morality is the device of the dwarf, another way of turning aside from our own existence as part of this endlessly fresh universe. The world is too deep for morality to grasp it.

---

ZARATHUSTRA'S BOOK OF ETERNAL RETURN

Origins are limitless: each thing has infinite new beginnings

---

Zarathustra swiftly confronts another adversary, which he calls rationality. This is another way of reducing the scale of the universe. Rationality is the faculty which seeks to understand everything in terms of human logic, cause and effect, purpose. In this sense, rationality is an ally of the dwarf, a way of shrinking the universe. How could any one way of thinking possibly be large enough to comprehend the infinite universe which appears at the gateway? Why should all things be tied down by one set of laws, why should the whole dance be performed to a single tune?

Zarathustra is not an irrationalist. He concedes that there is 'a little reasonableness' everywhere in the universe. It is as if that were a kind of snare, laid to make rationality over-confident. There is always a part of any situation that is accessible to reason. In other words, we can always explain something in terms of causes and effects, of purposes being pursued or foiled. It is just that there are always an infinite number of other things that defy such explanation, that demand a different interpretation.

> ZARATHUSTRA'S BOOK OF ETERNAL RETURN
>
> The universe is always partly rational, but a larger part is not rational

**PART III**
*'Of virtue that diminisheth'*

In the satisfaction of expounding and expanding, Zarathustra then seems to enter into his own happiness. He imagines himself confronting the world as 'Zarathustra the Godless!', defying all the respectable 'teachers' and outraging their docile audiences. The contrast here is with the beginning of *TSZ*, where Zarathustra wearily recalled the old stale message that 'God is dead', and smiled wryly at the old saint who had not yet noticed. Now we have the same idea, but understood from the centre of a personal world. There is the world of a difference between the old message and this active experience of being godless. But the echo is also disturbing. Has Zarathustra himself moved in a circle, coming back to the earlier state in which he was less capable of contact and communication, more wrapped in his own theory than able to influence others?

**PART III**
*'On the Mount of Olives'*

At the start of Part III, Zarathustra discovered his personal metaphor for experience, mountaineering. Now he climbs the mountain of biblical Christianity. There is a strong biblical feeling to the whole text, and it grows even stronger after the proclamation of eternal return. Zarathustra now argues that everything which comes into existence must have an infinite number of causes. That is why there can be only a little seed of reason in everything. But if there are infinite causes of each thing, then it can be endlessly recreated. If one cause is absent, there will always be another. The doctrine of eternal return is, therefore, at heart a theory of origins.

ZARATHUSTRA'S BOOK OF ETERNAL RETURN

There can be no first cause: infinite recurrence means endless causes

Zarathustra certainly demonstrates the many uses of the doctrine of eternal return. He draws conclusions in every direction, dizzying, radical, staggering even now. Yet is this still the same process of therapeutic philosophy? Or does the hardening of the central doctrine bring the therapy – and the education – to an end?

# 6 The Final Ambiguity

## THE FINAL PHASE
In this chapter, we look at the last sections of Part III and Part IV. Now the main theories have been presented, the nature of the book changes once again. We enter the phase of the final ambiguity, when all these ideas are again called into question.

## MANY HAPPY RETURNS?

> PART III
> *'Of apostates'*

Zarathustra comes upon his disciples once more, and the phase of the final reactions has begun. There is an energizing moment, an instant of anger, as he realizes that he is being betrayed, as others have been before by their disciples. The disciples declare that they have 'grown pious' again. Zarathustra rounds on them, with the scornful rebuke: '*Prayer is shameful.*' The return of prayer takes him back to the world of the saint, the world which he turned aside from in order to begin the therapeutic and philosophical quest of the book.

What does it mean, this new praying?

* First, it is the retreat to other-centredness, the refusal to live as and from 'I'.

* Second, it is the retreat from communication, into the non-communication of ritual.

This is a vision of modern history. For each breakthrough, each moment of advance, there will be a retreat.

| PART III      | So Zarathustra returns to his cave after he has |
| 'Home-coming' | |

So Zarathustra returns to his cave after he has re-met the disciples and seen them re-find their faith, and recovered his anger. He now recovers his own sense of solitary wisdom, which is where this phase of the journey began. We have an extraordinary vision of language itself. Zarathustra feels every word 'open suddenly', and yield its meaning afresh. It is as if the world were rushing towards words, demanding to be expressed. Everything wants to be made into Zarathustra's speech. There is an extraordinary sense of returning to the first moment, the moment when the desire to communicate arose. This is, then, a positive moment of repetition – to set against the negative moment of the return of faith among the disciples, the apostates.

| PART III          | Zarathustra then returns to his own inner |
| 'Of the Spirit of | |
| Gravity' II       | |

Zarathustra then returns to his own inner crisis: after the return of ecstasy, the return of illness. He re-encounters the Spirit of Gravity. Why is man endlessly beset by sickness, why is well-being never final? Zarathustra has a vision of the roots of our ill-being. If life is a quest for treasure, then the last buried treasure we will ever find is our own hoard. Each of us will unearth every other hoard, before finding our own buried riches.

What is it that hides our own treasure from us? It is language itself, or a false version of language, 'heavy words' of good and evil. We insist on speaking in these categories and so we can never dig down into our own riches. These words cut us off from what is richest in our own nature.

In other words, we stand at the gateway, choosing between the comforts of good and evil, and the riches of our own buried being. There is an element of despair about this repetition. Recovery is impossible, if by recovery is meant a final entry into well-being. The illness will always come back. But then again, the cure is also always possible. In Zarathustra, therapeutic philosophy confronts its own limitation.

---

FINAL AMBIGUITY: THERAPEUTIC PHILOSOPHY

Both sickness and cure must recur endlessly.

---

| P A R T   I I I |
| --- |
| *'Of old and new law-tables'* |

Zarathustra re-enters his own memories. He recalls the mission we have been following. What has he taught? He insists on his inner message. He is the teacher who demanded that his pupils become creators, that they remake their own past. He was the one who made the new rule: redeem the past, seize hold of it with your will. But now that teaching has become a recurring memory, itself an aspect of the past.

The lesson is never finished. The message has never been communicated. Just as the sickness will return endlessly, so the answer must find new life over and over again.

---

FINAL AMBIGUITY

We are always on the point of both relapse and recovery.

---

| P A R T   I I I |
| --- |
| *'The convalescent'* |

So we come to a section where Zarathustra experiences again his own breakdown. He lies for seven days of delirium on his bed, watched by his caring animals. Then he springs from his bed and speaks in a strange voice, as if the words belonged to someone else. The animals ask him to recover again and then they explain to him his own philosophy, beginning with the idea of return and repetition. Remember, they tell him, everything returns again. Zarathustra teases them in reply, fondly calling them his 'hurdy gurdies' (or 'barrel organs' in Hollingdale): endlessly repeating to him his own message.

This is a strange scene. Every aspect of it expresses in its own way the idea of endless repetition. The philosophy itself is being repeated all over the place. The animals remind the teacher that his essential lesson is this vision of eternal return. He in turn is re-experiencing both breakdown and recovery. He teases them with being mere mechanical repeaters of his original music. They respond by recalling him to his own identity:

QUOTATION

*'For thy beasts well know, O Zarathustra, what thou art and must become. Behold, thou art the Teacher of Eternal Recurrence ...'*

cross reference P: 237; V: 332

Nothing is more important about the last phase of *TSZ* than its strangeness. That seems to be its meaning. In this dream-like scene, the animals tell Zarathustra that he must return endlessly to being the teacher of endless return.

This stands for the whole nature of the ending. On the one hand, the book is utterly and uniquely consistent. Nothing is allowed which does not reflect this central idea of return. On the other hand, there is something absurd about this consistency. It seeks to go beyond anything rational or reasonable, into a kind of delirium itself.

FINAL AMBIGUITY

Eternal return is both cure and sickness, therapy and poison.

## THE PSYCHOLOGY OF ETERNAL RETURN

Part III ends with visions – especially 'the seven seals', which is itself a repetition of the Book of Revelation: a hymn to eternity, to cycles. Part IV then moves on through time: '*And once again months and years passed over.*' Zarathustra meets the last characters. They have all come to find him. These are the 'higher men', the ones who now need his help.

**The soothsayer**    He comes as a tempter, to force Zarathustra to feel pity for the lost world. This is the rival and the companion. He wants to drag Zarathustra back into the world of compassion, the world of values which he has denied. How can Zarathustra not feel sorry for all the suffering? A cry of anguish is heard: who could resist the lure of pity? This then is a first repetition of the old values. They will never disappear. Pity will remain an endless temptation, you will never break its hold.

> PART IV
> '*The cry for help*'

**The two kings**    They embody false authority. Through his forest come these two kings with their ass. They are suffocated by disgust at their own nature, at their falseness. They want to be redeemed by Zarathustra. He replies, saying how glad he is that they are so disgusted by their own authority. And then the kings are happy. They say how glad they are that they came to find this healer. There is something sinister about this moment. They begin to babble, to mutter in their own contentment. This seems to be a key moment where the book mocks its own therapeutic mission. It was their anxiety and disgust that made the kings worthy of response. Now that they feel they have been helped, they become once again sealed off, unaware of the world, incommunicatively happy.

> PART IV
> '*Conversation with kings*'

**The leech**    Next, Zarathustra walks through his forest until he accidentally steps on someone. This is an expert, a conscientious researcher on leeches.

> PART IV
> '*The leech*'

He is the spirit of scholarly knowledge. He knows absolutely everything about his speciality. Zarathustra asks what it is, this special subject. Is it the leech that this man knows all about? Oh no, replies the trodden-upon expert, the leech is far too large a field. He knows all about one organ: the leeches' brain. In his desire to know all about this brain, he refuses to know anything else in the world. He cannot afford to waste his research on trivia. He needs to focus entirely on this one chosen field, to have any chance of understanding it. Zarathustra points this man the way to his cave. The conscientious man stands for the sickness of knowledge itself, the enchantment of expertise. He is wrapped in the desire to know something finally. This too is an endless sickness: the enchantment of absolute knowledge.

**The wizard**  Next comes a man full of sorrowful self-pity, the

> PART IV
> 'The wizard'

wizard. He sings a dreadful lyric of misery and complaint. Zarathustra drives him with a stick into his cave. The sorcerer has the magic power of converting everything in his life into another source of misery.

**The old pope**  Then we find the last pope in the forest. He has

> PART IV
> 'Out of work'

abandoned his church, at last, and now comes to find the godless Zarathustra. There is a kind of terrible irony about this pope. He has replaced his need for God with his need for Zarathustra. This says something about the plight of the therapeutic philosopher. He has tried to liberate the world from its old faith, its attachment to external guarantees, its 'other-centredess'. But dependence is endlessly reborn – now the pope needs Zarathustra himself.

This final sequence can be understood in terms of a psychoanalytic concept that was developed soon after by Freud. In analysis, Freud said, the patient projects onto the blank sheet of the analyst his or her own deepest need, his or her own lost relationship. Freud's term for this repetition was 'transference'. Here, each character projects his need onto Zarathustra. The prophet demands pity from him; the kings want their authority back; the leech wants to be assured that he is indeed a great expert; the sorcerer wants to sing his song of misery to an appreciative audience; the old pope wants a new ideal. Zarathustra, who tried to bring the truth, becomes for each of these characters the personification of their own deepest need. This is the most ironic return or repetition: the characters project onto Zarathustra the very need from which he has tried to free them. But like the Freudian analyst, Zarathustra then has to try again.

---

PART IV
'*The ugliest man*'

---

The carnival continues. After the lost pope comes his opposite, **the ugliest man**: he is the one who expresses guilt. This man is convinced that he was the one who killed God. The pope is beset by a feeling of loss and unfulfilled mourning; the ugliest man is beset by the despair of endless guilt. Each remains trapped in an endlessly repeating emotion. Zarathustra sends the ugliest man to his cave with the others.

---

FINAL AMBIGUITY

**The cave**

This cave is partly itself a repetition of Plato's cave. In *The Republic*, the human condition is seen as a cave, where each person is kept prisoner, watching shadows dance on the walls. This philosopher's cave is in a way the reverse; a home of truth rather than illusion.

* The cave is also the place of refuge.

* The cave is the womb, the place of beginning.

* The cave is the goal, the ending.

---

**The voluntary beggar** follows the ugliest man. He is the one who

| PART IV |
|---|
| *'The voluntary beggar'* |

personifies the sickness of endless giving. Zarathustra himself seemed to suffer from this condition, earlier. The beggar has been unable to resist the lure of generosity. It has left him empty, as at times it seems to leave Zarathustra himself. It begins to look as if each of these sick figures represents partly an aspect of Zarathustra. He could have become any one of them. He could, for instance, have been a conscientious expert, or a misery-singing sorcerer, or a last pope, or a guilt-ridden murderer. These characters can also be interpreted as repetitions or returns of Zarathustra's own impulses.

Finally, then, there must be **the shadow**. This last figure represents

| PART IV |
|---|
| *'The shadow'* |

Zarathustra's own other self. The shadow is the spirit of his teachings, but distorted into a kind of sickness. Here Zarathustra is a searcher, the shadow is homeless. What Zarathustra experiences as freedom, the shadow feels as loss.

The final part of *TSZ* seems to converge profoundly with the spirit of twentieth-century psychology. Transference, shadow, the unconscious: these concepts seem to be implicit in the last events of the book. Therapeutic philosophy is actually remaking itself into modern psychoanalysis in these last episodes.

## ZARATHUSTRA'S MODERNITY

### JUNG AND THE SHADOW

In the psychology of Carl Gustav Jung, each of us has a shadow self, which is a projection of everything left out of our usual self. Zarathustra's shadow expresses his own suppressed fears and longings.

ZARATHUSTRA AND PSYCHOANALYSIS

**The psychology of eternal return**

Nothing ever goes away, in human experience. This seems to be the affinity between *TSZ* and psychoanalytic thought. All the suppressed fears are still there, in the shadow self. All the old needs are still present, waiting to be expressed in new ways.

You never break the hold of the old emotions; but equally, you never lose the hope of recovering once more.

## THE LAST SUPPER

| PART IV |
|---|
| *'The salutation'* |

The characters gather in Zarathustra's cave. It is noon, and hot. He laughs at them, as they bow respectfully to him. Then begins a dream-like finale. Zarathustra repeats his teaching, that they are all weighed down by the past, that they need to lighten the grip of memory on their being. But then again, that too is a repetition.

| PART IV |
|---|
| *'The supper'* |

The soothsayer demands dinner. This is another moment of parody – of the biblical last supper, and also of Zarathustra's own life – here he is in the cave, and what do they want? Something to eat. More giving-away. Through the dialogue, we hear the kings' ass braying happily – a travesty of affirmation and recovery of self-being.

| PART IV |
|---|
| *'Of the higher man'* |

Zarathustra is drawn to repeat his own stories. He recalls his first failure as a teacher in the marketplace. He reminds everyone of his doctrines and discoveries. He even repeats the theme of the superman, which has not been heard of for some time. He then slips out of the door into the garden. A weird dialogue arises among the guests. The wizard tries to seduce them all into his own misery with a song. The conscientious expert is the one who can resist the lure.

He produces a theory of why they have all sought out Zarathustra – they have opposing needs. He, the expert, wants more security; the sorcerer wants to be more insecure.

> P A R T   I V
> *'Of science'*

This is a carnival of theories and ideas. The guests become a travesty of philosophical dialogue. They all have their viewpoint, they are full of arguments. They debate at a high level, while at the same time, they are all waiting for Zarathustra who must bring them the answer, the cure.

> P A R T   I V
> *'The awakening'*

Zarathustra comes back – another return, of course. He finds his guests happy, and in disgust and mockery he realizes that they have found new faith. They are once again at prayer, to their own well-being. He hears the 'Hee-Haw Yea!' of the ass. It stands for the absurd side of recovery and wellness, 'The Feast of the Ass'. Dispute breaks out, as Zarathustra attacks those who have returned to cosy certainty. In their different ways, the guests – the higher men – justify their clinging to fragments of religious faith. This finale is a kind of glimpse of a future where religion has survived as a sneaky support, a not-quite-acknowledged defence mechanism. The leech, for example, speaks under the name of 'the most conscientious one', the spirit of intellectual rigour. He wriggles off Zarathustra's hook, by insisting that he does not actually 'believe' in God, but finds the deity 'credible'.

> P A R T   I V
> *'The drunken song'*

The whole journey ends with a moment of ambiguous release for Zarathustra, a song of ecstasy and despair, a final vision and a collapse:

---

QUOTATION

*O drunken midnight's death-joy, singing: The world is deep,* and deeper than every day may deem!

cross reference P: 330; V: 433

# Conclusion:
# The Spirit of Zarathustra

Writing after the Second World War, the eminent Hungarian Marxist Georg Lukacs identified Nietzsche as 'the philosopher of Fascism'. More cautiously, the German novelist Thomas Mann suggested that while it was untrue 'that Nietzsche created Fascism', it was true 'the Fascism created him'. Mann meant that the anxieties of the Fascist period were already finding expression in the writings of the late nineteenth-century thinker.

His association with the Nazi period has certainly coloured the entire reception of all of Nietzsche's works, including especially *TSZ*. Reviewing Nietzsche's after-life, Tracey Strong ('Nietzsche's Political Misappropriation', *The Cambridge Companion to Nietzsche*, 1996 pp. 119–50) establishes the central problem: '*It is well known that National Socialism claimed to find its roots*' in some of his main ideas. These include key elements of *TSZ*, particularly 'the superman', which was reinterpreted as a slogan for the destiny of the German nation. Concepts such as 'the superman' and 'the will' certainly became part of the vocabulary of Nazism, and Nietzsche served to give some sort of respectability or lineage to the rhetoric.

Ernst Behler tells the story of Nietzsche's fate in the twentieth century. The major source used by the Nazi commentators tended to be a volume published under the heading *The Will to Power*, in which Elisabeth, Nietzsche's sister, collected together unpublished notebooks from his later years. In 1931, Alfred Baumler published an influential account of Nietzsche as the philosopher of 'the will to power'. As we have seen in context, the will is an extremely subtle concept in *TSZ*. But this sense of Nietzsche as the thinker who endorses the pursuit of power was useful at the time. Later times have recovered Nietzsche's more subtle sense of will and his more critical, appreciation of power, but his negative reputation, in Anglophone countries particularly, derives from this Fascist appropriation.

The most important thinker of the Nazi period was the philosopher Martin Heidegger, whose *Being and Time* (1927) continues to play an important role in current philosophical discussion. Heidegger was a member of the Nazi party and, in this period, he was also the Rector of the University of Marburg, an influential figure to begin with on Nazi ideas of education. This influence soon waned, but Heidegger continued in the Party through the war. In these years, Heidegger gave a series of lectures on Nietzsche. Controversy rages about Heidegger as philosopher and as associate of the Nazis. These lectures certainly played their part in making the link between Nietzsche and Fascism but, on the other hand, his biographer Rudiger Safranski notes that Heidegger also had far more complex things to say about his German predecessor.

As Behler ('Nietzsche in the Twentieth Century', *The Cambridge Companion to Nietzsche*, especially pp. 311–15) demonstrates, Zarathustra is an important text for Heidegger because he took extremely seriously Nietzsche's theory of eternal return. Heidegger argued that Nietzsche had not himself correctly understood this major concept and he devoted great energy to reworking it. In particular, he wanted to make a closer connection between the two concepts of eternal return and will (to power). Heidegger claimed that these formed 'one thought' and that they together expressed for the first time 'the essence of modernity.' Heidegger declared that: '*In the essential unity of the two thoughts, the metaphysics that is approaching culmination utters its final word.*'

Heidegger believed that Nietzsche had failed to unify his own thinking about the human condition. He had not made the true connection between ingredients like will and eternal return. Had he done so, he would have been the prophet of the new age. As it was, that role had passed to Nietzsche's reinterpreter, Heidegger himself!

Heidegger also dwelt on the famous declaration that 'God is dead!' in a famous essay 'The Word of Nietzsche: God is dead!'. Here Heidegger argued that Nietzsche was in fact a fully incorporated member of the tradition which he wished to break. He belongs, for Heidegger, 'in the unbroken path of tradition'. It is only with the advent of Heidegger and his new age that such sentences can take on their proper meaning. Again, Heidegger – unlike the simpler propagandists – is aware that Nietzsche does not fit with his purposes. He claims not to interpret Nietzsche, so much as to refashion his key ideas so that they realized a new meaning. It is only with the violent intervention of Heidegger's authority that Nietzsche can be wrenched from his place and made to serve the interests of the would-be new age.

In the same period, as we have seen, Karl Jaspers produced his antidote to the Nazi claim on Nietzsche. Here too *TSZ* was central. For Jaspers, Zarathustra represented a Nietzschean ideal, but it was the very opposite of the Nazi slogans of superman and domination. Jaspers found in Zarathustra the central example of Nietzsche's belief in communication, a vision for which '*strength resides solely in a sort of openness*'. Zarathustra is an anti-totalitarian symbol, for Jaspers, a man who seeks to open his mind to others, even at the greatest cost to himself. Jaspers also found a certain tension in this Zarathustra, a tension between '*prophetic proclamation and rejection of blind followers*'. In the shadow of Hitler, this is a liberating tension. Zarathustra is the one who could be – but refuses to be – a demagogue. He has the eloquence at his disposal, the stirring themes and the power to attract followers. But instead of making his audience blind, he seeks to open their eyes to their own responsibility.

Jaspers found in *TSZ* a deep humanism, a resistance to any systems or ideals that are not rooted in human experience. Nietzsche was the philosopher in whom humanism found its climax, the voice who demanded an '*affirmation of man just as he is with all his possibilities*'. In this context, the superman is the central symbol of 'an appeal for further self-development'. On the other hand, Jaspers was bitterly dismissive of the idea of eternal return. Conceived in the face of Nazism, his Zarathustra is understandably rationalized – the mystical or even mysterious aspects are too risky at that moment.

Jaspers and Heidegger were originally friends. Their conflicting views form part of the cultural conflict of the Nazi period. They also belong more generally to the history of Existentialism. Through the earlier twentieth century, Nietzsche was increasingly seen as the key figure in the development of modern existentialist thought, a movement famously associated with Sartre, on the Left, and Heidegger, on the Right. This philosophy was rooted, in all its versions, in 'the question of being' – a rejection of all categories that seek to come before bare existence. There is no meaning to the human condition before we give it our own significance. *TSZ* was an important aspect of this existential Nietzsche, and particularly because of its blend of philosophy and fiction that anticipated the work of Sartre, Camus and de Beauvoir.

After the war, this more humanist existential account of Nietzsche was sustained by Walter Kaufman, who also provided one of the major translations of *TSZ*. Perhaps because of the associations with Fascist rhetoric, there has been a tendency in post-war versions to make the voices as conversational as possible. The biblical tenor of the earlier versions may have been overdone, but perhaps the pendulum has swung too far the other way in these later translations.

However, another major phase of Nietzsche's intellectual influence was still to come. From the 1960s onwards, his ideas were reinterpreted in the new theories of philosophers and critics including Jacques Derrida, Michel Foucault and the postmodernists Jean-François Lyotard and Jean Baudrillard.

This anti-authoritarian, radical Nietzsche is especially important in the work of Foucault, theorist of prisons and institutional oppression. Foucault follows through Nietzsche's critique of morality as worked out in *TSZ* and other later works such as *Genealogy of Morals* and *Beyond Good and Evil*. He develops a whole historical chronicle out of Nietzsche's critique of punishment and reward that we have seen in *TSZ*. However, the deeper influence is from Nietzsche's idea of eternal return, which becomes for Foucault a working principle rather than an image of human consciousness in time.

In his famous essay 'Nietzsche, Genealogy and History', Foucault develops Nietzsche's genealogy of morals idea – the tracing of the family histories of the oppressive concepts and values of western society. He sees in moral values a bundle of feelings, sentiments and associations. Foucault warns that to write the history of such values and their elements one must give up on the dream of a single origin. Instead the critic must train his gaze to notice these feelings, phrases and attitudes and develop a method that '*must be sensitive to their recurrence, not in order to trace the gradual course of their evolution, but to isolate the different scenes where they were engaged*'. Genealogy is about recurrence. Foucault also takes up Nietzsche's associated image of 'the moment' here. He wants to replace a linear story with a series of moments understood as different yet linked recurrences of the moral elements of the West.

Perhaps, however, the most well-known of all post-60s re-readings of *TSZ* is contained in a novel – Milan Kundera's *The Unbearable Lightness of Being*. This is a deeply anti-totalitarian novel, set around the Soviet invasion of Kundera's Czechoslovakia in 1968. It is also a work of philosophical reflection, which begins with 'the idea of eternal return'. The novel finds this concept 'mysterious' and even sees it as a 'mad myth'. At the same time, Kundera bases his fiction on the ambiguity of eternal return, both the 'heaviest of burdens' and our 'most intense fulfilment'. Eternal return is the alternative to 'unbearable lightness': the image of a world where our experience has weight. More subtly, Kundera has recreated the entire ambiguity of *TSZ*: fiction and philosophy, myth and rational argument, prophecy and protest. Despite past distortions, the spirit of Zarathustra continues to perplex and liberate.

# REFERENCES AND FURTHER READING

Derrida, Jacques, *Spurs: Nietzsche's Styles*, translated by Barbara Harlow (Chicago University Press, 1979).

Foucault, Michel, 'Nietzsche, Genealogy, History' in Paul Rabinow (ed.), *The Foucault Reader* (Penguin, 1991).

Hayman, Ronald, *Nietzsche: A Critical Life* (Weidenfeld & Nicolson, 1980).

Hollingdale, R. J. *Nietzsche: The Man and His Philosophy* (Cambridge University Press, 1999).

Jaspers, Karl, *Nietzsche*, translated by Charles F. Wallcraft and Frederick J. Schmitz (Johns Hopkins University Press, 1997).

Kundera, Milan, *The Unbearable Lightness of Being*, translated by Michael Henry Heim (faber & faber, 1985).

Lampart, Laurence, *Nietzsche's Teaching* (Yale University Press, 1986)

Magus, Bernd and Higgins, Kathleen M., *The Cambridge Companion to Nietzsche* (Cambridge University Press, 1996), notably essays by Tracey B. Strong and Ernst Behler.

Nussbaum, Martha C., *Love's Knowledge: Essays on Philosophy and Literature* (Oxford University Press, 1990).

Pearson, Keith Ansell, *Viroid Life: Perspectives on Nietzsche and the Transhuman Condition* (Routledge, 1997).

Safranski, Rudiger, *Martin Heidegger*, translated by Ewald Osers (Harvard University Press, 1998).

Beyond the editions cited at the start, further Nietzsche references are from:

Nietzsche, Friedrich, *Human, All Too Human* , translated by R.J. Hollingdale (Cambridge University Press, 1986).

Nietzsche, Friedrich, *Untimely Meditations*, translated by R.J.Hollingdale (Cambridge University Press, 1983).

# INDEX